RMS LUSITANIA:

THE STORY OF A WRECK

TAKE UP THE SWORD OF JUSTICE

RMS LUSITANIA:
THE STORY OF A WRECK

Exploring the Wreck 100 Years On:
Mapping, Protecting & Commemorating

**Fionnbarr Moore, Connie Kelleher, Karl Brady,
Charise McKeon, Ian Lawler**

With contributions by

Seán Kirwan, Nessa O'Connor, Commandant (Ret.) Peter Daly,
Captain Michael McCarthy, Laurence Dunne, Stewart Andrews,
Pat Coughlan, Roy Stokes and James Lyttleton

© Government of Ireland 2019

BAILE ÁTHA CLIATH
ARNA FHOILSIÚ AG OIFIG AN tSOLÁTHAR
Le ceannach díreach ón
OIFIG DHÍOLTA FOILSEACHÁN RIALTAIS.
52 FAICHE STIABHNA, BAILE ÁTHA CLIATH 2
Teil. 01–6476834 nó glaoch áitiúil: 1890 213434, FACS. 01–6476843;
Riomhphost: publications@opw.ie nó trí aon díoltóir leabhar.

DUBLIN
PUBLISHED BY THE STATIONERY OFFICE
To be purchased directly from the
GOVERNMENT PUBLICATIONS SALES OFFICE,
52 ST STEPHEN'S GREEN, DUBLIN 2,
Tel. 01–6476834 or LoCall: 1890 213434, FAX 01–6476843;
Email: publications@opw.ie or through any bookseller.

ISBN: 978-1-5272-0772-1

Design and production: Katrina Bouchier, Environmental Publications
Cover design: Conor Gallagher, Eyecon Design Consultants
Copy-editor: Sheelagh Hughes, Editorial Solutions Ireland Ltd.
Index: Julitta Clancy
Printer: GPS Colour Graphics Ltd.

Price €20

Half title page: A few months after the sinking of the *Lusitania* the German satirical medallist Karl Goetz produced a medal intended to castigate the British for their disregard for possible civilian casualties in sending the *Lusitania* through a 'war zone'. Unfortunately for Goetz, he took the date of the sinking from an incorrect news report and as a result the medal bears the date 5th May, instead of 7th May. Inevitably, the British acquired a copy and over 300,000 copies were produced, along with a leaflet explaining that this was proof of Germany's intention to sink the *Lusitania*, without any regard for the possible loss of non-combatants' lives. (Ian Lawler Collection)

Frontispiece: Recruitment poster issued by the Parliamentary Recruiting Committee in London, June 1915, following the sinking of the *Lusitania*. The poster shows a woman rising from the sea offering a sword with which to exact retribution. The *Lusitania* can be seen sinking in the background along with some of the drowning victims. (Courtesy of the Library of Congress, Prints & Photographs Division)

Contents

SECTION 4

Dedication

To all who lost their lives on the RMS *Lusitania*
Go raibh suaimhneas agaibh, go raibh beannacht libh
agus go gcuimhnítear oraibh go brách.

Detail from *Lusitania* Monument in Cobh, County Cork. Designed and sculpted by internationally renowned sculptor Jerome Connor (1874–1945). Connor won a prestigious competition in 1925 from the *Lusitania* Peace Memorial Committee in New York to design a monument commemorating the lives lost in the sinking of the RMS *Lusitania* (see www.buildingsofireland.ie for more detail). Initiated by Bert Hubbard, whose parents Elbert and Alice Hubbard lost their lives in the sinking, the commission was also financially supported by Gertrude Vanderbilt Whitney, whose brother Alfred also perished when the *Lusitania* sank. Casting finally began in 1936 but with the outbreak of World War Two, Connor went bankrupt and sadly died before its full completion. Following representation in 1965 by sculptor Domhnall O'Murchada, Assistant Professor of Sculptor in the National College of Art, the monument was finally completed in 1968 through the work of local sculptor Fred Conlon (1943–2005). (Photo by Connie Kelleher)

Wreck of Ages

Decades deep, decades past,
Structure crumbles but stories last.
Dark shadow beneath the waves,
Sunken monument of countless graves.
That never fades.

Eighteen minutes that changed worlds,
So ended lives, and began quarrels;
Of wars and men and rights and wrongs,
Of books and posters, films and songs.
That goes on and on.

Dive the depth, shine a light
Peer and see a familiar sight:
Bollards, chains, deck and hold,
The dulled brass of displaced portholes.
Through which stare invisible souls.

Lonely lady lost at sea
Fascination is your legacy.
Ocean's living arcadia
Ponder that, pro memoria.

Wreck of Ages, *Lusitania*.
(© C. Kelleher, 2017)

Foreword

Over the few short years of World War I, nearly one thousand vessels were lost off Irish shores. The sinking of the passenger liner RMS *Lusitania* during this period is one of the best known and evocative. Against a background of tremendous loss of life, the story of the *Lusitania* continues to inspire debate among the academic community and the general public. Meanwhile, the imposing wreck, which has lain below the Atlantic Ocean for over 100 years, is a physical monument to the devastation that occurred at sea.

Over the past decade collaborative work between my Department's National Monuments Service, the Geological Survey Ireland and the Marine Institute on a programme of surveying, mapping, recording and interpreting shipwreck sites around the coast, has greatly informed our extensive database of shipwrecks – to date over 18,000 wrecks have been documented around Irish shores. My Department has a statutory role in the management and protection of our underwater cultural heritage, including mandatory protection of all wrecks over 100 years old. Last year's centenary of the World War I armistice marked the entry into statutory protection of the last of the many wrecks lost during that conflict.

Since the sinking of the RMS *Lusitania* in 1915 with the loss of almost 1,200 souls, several expeditions have been undertaken to the wreck site, by salvors, researchers and recreational divers. The *Lusitania's* significance to history is such that in 1995, in accordance with heritage legislation, an underwater heritage order was placed on the wreck, ensuring that expeditions are now regulated in terms of heritage impact.

Reports from diver expeditions on the wreck of the *Lusitania* over the past two decades, in tandem with results from surveys carried out over the wreck since 2002, continue to add to our understanding of the site. Such research informs long-term management strategies for the wreck site and the development of appropriate avenues of investigation for its exploration, in keeping with best international practice. It is particularly reassuring to me that any future explorations will also have the benefit of proceeding on the basis of the Memorandum of Understanding drawn up in 2013 between my Department and the owner of the *Lusitania*, Mr. F. Gregg Bemis Jr.

This publication on RMS *Lusitania* continues the excellent collaboration between the National Monuments Service, the Geological Survey Ireland and the Marine Institute, not only in telling the story of the wreck itself but also of the World War I losses generally off our coast. By enriching the insights of historians, archaeologists, divers and associated specialists with the results of seabed mapping, the story of the *Lusitania* is presented here in a new way. This book vividly recreates the imposing and dramatic nature of the wreck as it exists today on the seabed, while also providing a better understanding of the events that led to its sinking and the consequences that followed from it.

The story of the wreck of RMS *Lusitania* continues to occupy a central position in debate about a crucial period of modern European history. This book is a timely contribution to knowledge about both the wreck itself and the context in which it sank.

Josepha Madigan

Josepha Madigan TD
Minister for Culture, Heritage and the Gaeltacht

Preface

For the past 18 years, Ireland's offshore waters and coastal seas have been subject to one of the largest seabed surveys in the world. Integrated Mapping for the Sustainable Development of Ireland's Marine Resource (INFOMAR) is Ireland's national marine mapping programme, the follow-on project to the Irish National Seabed Survey (INSS) which began in 1999. The project is a joint venture of the Geological Survey Ireland, Department of Communications, Climate Action and Environment and the Marine Institute, Department of Agriculture, Food and the Marine.

INFOMAR concentrates on creating a range of integrated mapping products of the physical features of the seabed in the near-shore area, and provides this data for free. Such a data delivery strategy is intended to promote value-added products and contribute to the national development effort, and to our future socio-economic prosperity. This data is also being incorporated into various EC projects generating new datasets on a European level, to inform planning decisions at the highest levels.

Since the beginning of the INSS in 1999 a comprehensive database of the shipwrecks that have been mapped around the coast of Ireland has been collected. It is this dataset that has provided in-depth information of known and previously unknown shipwrecks in Irish waters and has led to collaborative work with the National Monuments Service's Underwater Archaeology Unit (Department of Culture, Heritage and the Gaeltacht). The mapped data has, in most cases, greatly improved the accuracy of the charted position for many of these shipwrecks, some of which are world renowned, as well as providing never before seen images of how these shipwrecks lie on the seafloor today.

Since 2002 a number of surveys have been carried out on the site of the RMS *Lusitania* through the work of the INFOMAR project. This publication reveals that state-of-the-art sonar imagery of the wreck, the most detailed information and overview compiled to date. The 2014 survey of the wreck site acquired imagery that continues to enlighten us on the nature and extent of the remains on the seabed while also providing us with a tangible link to the wreck and its loss over 100 years ago.

This collection of data, and the story of the wreck, present greater detail on the ship, its history and its loss. Furthermore, it provides us with a platform upon which new research and analysis can be based. This new survey data is extremely important from a site protection point of view. It will add to our knowledge and understanding of the wreck site on the seabed, its current condition and how the site has changed or degraded over the years. Such a dataset will contribute significantly to the management and protection measures in place for Ireland's marine cultural heritage and also to the safety of navigation in Irish waters.

Sean Canney

Sean Canney TD
Minister of State at the Department of Rural and Community Development and Department of Communications, Climate Action and Environment.

Acknowledgements

This publication is the result of ongoing collaboration between the National Monuments Service and the Geological Survey Ireland in mapping, analysing and interpreting survey data gathered on the wreck of the RMS *Lusitania* during the Irish National Seabed Survey and the INFOMAR (the INtegrated Mapping FOr the Sustainable Development of Ireland's MARine Resource) mapping projects. The state-of-the-art time-lapse multibeam imagery of the wreck of *Lusitania* would not have been made possible without the hard work of the various surveyors, data processors and crews on board the SV *Bligh*, RV *Celtic Voyager* and RV *Keary*, who have been tirelessly mapping and surveying the Irish seabed since 1999 as part of the Irish National Seabed Survey and INFOMAR programmes. Minister Seán Canney of the Department of Communications, Climate Action and Environment and its predecessors and all previous Ministers and senior administrative staff are acknowledged for continuous support of the Irish National Seabed Survey and INFOMAR projects in mapping Ireland's seabed. Thanks are also due to all the staff, past and present, of INFOMAR and the Irish National Seabed Survey both from the Geological Survey Ireland and the Marine Institute. We wish to thank Koen Verbruggen, the Director of the Geological Survey Ireland, Sean Cullen, Project Manager of INFOMAR (Geological Survey Ireland), and Archie Donovan (former Project Manager of INFOMAR), for their support and encouragement for this publication.

The Department of Culture, Heritage and the Gaeltacht (DCHG) has a long-established role in managing and protecting Ireland's shipwreck heritage, including the remains of the *Lusitania*. The authors are delighted to be able to make available to the public this publication, which discusses the history and archaeology of the *Lusitania* and the issues surrounding its preservation. The support of the Minister for Culture, Heritage and the Gaeltacht, Josepha Madigan, T. D. and all previous ministers and senior administrative staff is acknowledged. Katherine Licken, Secretary General, Niall Ó Donnchú, Assistant Secretary General (DCHG), Terry Allen, Director of the National Monuments Service (NMS), Michael MacDonagh, Chief Archaeologist, Danielle McCormack and Muirne Lyons, have also supported the book to completion. The encouragement of previous NMS colleagues David Sweetman, Brian Duffy, Dr Ann Lynch, and Paul Walsh, is also gratefully acknowledged. The collaboration of colleagues at the National Museum of Ireland, and the wealth of expertise which they have generously shared over the years, is also much appreciated.

The authors of this book would like to acknowledge the contributions made by many individuals who have provided information on the remains of the wreck not just for this publication but over the years. Many people assisted in the compilation and production of the book in a number of ways: staff of the National Monuments Service who assisted at various levels with its production; contributions made by Commandant (Ret.) Peter Daly; Captain Michael McCarthy and Port of Cork; Cobh Heritage Lusitania Commemorations Committee; Cobh Heritage Centre and Cobh Museum; the late John Davis (Irish Shipping) for sharing his extensive knowledge of all things maritime; archaeologists Laurence Dunne and Julianna O'Donoghue; Caitríona Devane; the many divers who have engaged first hand with the wreck including Eoin McGarry, Pat Coughlan, Stewart Andrews, Timmy Carey, Barry McGill, Roy Stokes and Pat Glavin and their respective dive teams. Underwater archaeological colleagues Dave Ball and Melanie Damour of the Bureau of Ocean Energy Management (BOEM) in the United States provided relevant information on their Deep Water Wrecks Project and were always available to discuss new technologies and methodologies.

The National Monuments Service would also like to acknowledge the support of the office of the Receiver of Wreck, Customs and Excise, Revenue Service, in particular Gerry Greenway and Patrick O'Sullivan (both now retired), Joe Martin O'Sullivan, Customs Liaison Officer, MAOC-N, Lisbon, Portugal, and Receiver of Wreck for Cork, Michael Jones. The support of the Irish Naval Service is also acknowledged, particularly Commander Thomas Tuohy and Lt. Commander Brian Fitzgerald along with their colleagues Commander Cormac Rynne and Lt. Commander Conor Kirwan of the Naval Dive Unit, for their assistance with our inspections of licensed dives on the wreck.

We wish to thank President Michael D. Higgins for permission to reproduce the speech he delivered at the 100th Anniversary Commemorations in Cobh on 7th May 2015.

The interest shown over many years by the owner of the *Lusitania*, F. Gregg Bemis, in its history and in the questions surrounding its rapid sinking, and his ongoing commitment to its exploration are acknowledged by the Department of Culture, Heritage and the Gaeltacht.

Acknowledgements are also due to the following institutions for permission to publish copyrighted material: the National Library of Ireland; the National Museum of Ireland; the National Maritime Museum, Greenwich; the Imperial War Museum, London; Naval History and Heritage Command, Washington Navy Yard, Washington DC; the Library of Congress, Washington DC; An Post; *The Irish Examiner*; Ionad an Bhlascaoid Mhóir, Dunquin, County Kerry. Thanks are due to Dr Eugene Keane (formally of the Office of Public Works) for referring the authors to the image of the *Lusitania* deck chair on the Great Blasket Island. Sincere thanks also to the following individuals for contributing images: Ian Lawler; Laurence Dunne; Barry McGill; Dr Fabio Sacchetti of the Marine Institute and Dr Ruth Plets of the University of Ulster, Coleraine. Maritime artist Brian Cleare freely gave access to his many wonderful paintings of not only the *Lusitania* but also other ships from the period. Thanks must also be given to Tony Roche and John Lalor of National Monuments Service Photographic Unit for their help, supply of images and assistance with image-enhancement work. Final thanks are due to Katrina Bouchier at Environmental Publications for her excellent design work, typesetting skills and management of the production of this book, Conor Gallagher of Eyecon Design Consultants for his excellent design of the cover and to Sheelagh Hughes of Editorial Solutions Ireland Ltd. for her patience and outstanding editorial skills.

Seabed mapping image acknowledgements

All multibeam and sidescan sonar images used in the book are supplied by the Irish National Seabed Survey (Geological Survey Ireland) and INFOMAR (Geological Survey Ireland/Marine Institute), unless otherwise stated.

Opposite: Artist's interpretation on the cover of *Le Petit Journal* in 1922 illustrating how the wreck of the *Lusitania* might be investigated. (Ian Lawler Collection)

12 Pages   12 Pages

Le Petit Journal
illustré

HEBDOMADAIRE
61, rue Lafayette, Paris

PRIX : **0 fr. 30**
17 Décembre 1922

Sous la Mer

Imagine-t-on un être humain, revêtu d'une semblable carapace d'acier et de cuir et se mouvant dans les grandes profondeurs sous-marines ? Ces monstres ne semblent-ils pas créés par l'imagination d'un Jules Verne ou d'un Wells ? En réalité, ces scaphandres formidables sont employés par une société de renflouement, pour reconnaître l'épave du *Lusitania* coulé par 80 mètres de fond.

"There is no doubt that the *Lusitania* was one of the most beautiful liners ever built; its size, speed and opulence ensured that it made maritime history during its heyday crossing the Atlantic."

SECTION 1

Introduction

If the RMS *Titanic* had not hit an iceberg in 1912 and sunk in the deep, icy waters of the North Atlantic, the wreck of the Cunard ocean liner RMS *Lusitania* would almost certainly be the most famous shipwreck in the world. As it stands, it is one of the signal destination dive sites for recreational divers and the remains of the wreck, the story behind the sinking and the work that has taken place on the site over the intervening years since it sank in 1915, have been the focus of both public and private interest for decades; and so it continues.

The remains of the *Lusitania* lie at a depth of over 93m, 11.5 nautical miles off the south coast of Ireland and within sight of the Old Head of Kinsale. On 7th May 1915 the ship had almost completed a transatlantic voyage en route from New York to Liverpool when it was spotted by German submarine *U-20* under the command of *Kapitänleutnant* Walther Schwieger. One torpedo was fired, striking the liner on its starboard side but the exact location of the strike awaits confirmation. The torpedo strike may have triggered a secondary explosion, something which many survivors claimed to have heard, and this may have accelerated the ship's loss; it took just 18 minutes to sink fully beneath the waves. In his log, Walther Schwieger noted that he had fired one torpedo and that after the explosion caused by that torpedo there was almost immediately a second, larger explosion. Of 1,960 people on board, including three stowaways, 1,193 lives were lost on site and 767 were rescued, four of whom died later. The loss of 128 American citizens caused outrage in the United States and calls were made for the US to enter the war in Europe on the Allied side.

The wreck site is the last resting place of over 900 people, many of whose remains may still be entombed within the wreck itself. It therefore deserves to be afforded due respect as the mass grave site of those unfortunate passengers and crew – a point often overlooked by divers wishing to explore the wreck and its mysteries. Only 289 bodies were ever recovered; most of these were interred in the Old Church Cemetery in Cobh, though others were washed up along the coast from Kerry to Mayo and many of these individuals are buried in graveyards close to where they were found. Due to its historical and archaeological significance and cognisant of the fact that it is very much a war grave and should be protected as such, the Irish Government placed an Underwater Heritage Order on the wreck site in 1995. The Order was placed by the then Minister for Arts, Culture and the Gaeltacht (now President) Michael D. Higgins, and this had the effect of requiring anyone wishing to undertake diving or other intrusive investigations aimed at the exploration of the wreck site to apply to the Minister for a licence to do so. With the 100th anniversary of its sinking having passed in May 2015, the wreck is now also protected under the 100-year rule which protects all wrecks of that age or older.

The mid-1990s also saw the question of title to the wreck of the *Lusitania* receive formal consideration before the courts in Ireland, having previously been the subject of litigation in the United States and United Kingdom. Following an application made to the High Court by Mr F. Gregg Bemis, the High Court of Ireland granted a declaration that Mr Bemis was the "sole and exclusive owner of all rights, title and interest in the R.M.S. '*Lusitania*', her hull, tackle, appurtenances, engines and apparel". The application for the declaration, in the terms granted, was unchallenged by the State. The declaration did not cover the question of title to cargo and personal effects on board the wreck. (*Bemis v. Owners of R.M.S. "Lusitania"* 14th May 1996 IEHC 2.)

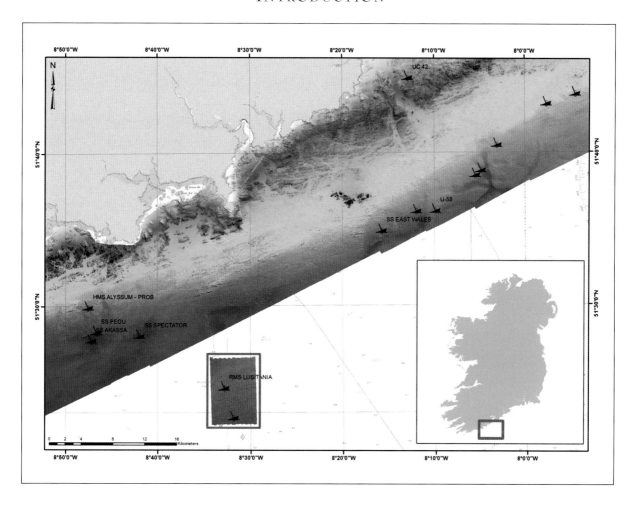

Above: The location of the RMS *Lusitania*, 22km (11.5nm) south of the Old Head of Kinsale. The area of seabed indicated by a red box in the main picture is protected by an Underwater Heritage Order under the 1987 National Monuments (Amendment) Act. This area was surveyed in detail by INFOMAR in 2014.

Multibeam view of the once magnificent liner lying on its starboard side, slowly collapsing in on itself. The bow of the ship is in the top right hand corner of the image with the stern in the bottom left. The wreck measures 241m long, 46m at its widest and has an average height of 9.9m.

O.T.S.S. LUSITANIA.

Previous page: Contemporary postcard of the *Lusitania*. The 31,550 GRT liner was considered to be not only the most luxurious ship when built but also the largest. It made 202 transatlantic crossings during its eight years in service. (Ian Lawler Collection)

One of two commemorative stamps issued by An Post in 2015 to mark the centenary of the sinking of the *Lusitania*. This stamp shows the *Lusitania* sinking bow first into the sea. (Reproduced by kind permission of An Post ©)

The implementation of the Underwater Heritage Order in circumstances where there is a known owner who is actively interested in the exploration of the wreck (as Mr Bemis is) has required the State and Mr Bemis to work together. This arrangement between the State and the owner of the wreck has not always been without disagreement as can be seen from the judicial review proceedings of the early 2000s (*Bemis v Minister for Arts, Heritage, Gaeltacht and the Islands and Ors*, High Court, Unreported decision of Herbert J. 17th June 2005; Supreme Court Unreported 27th March 2007). However, as is discussed later in this book, a working relationship between the parties has been developed which has facilitated ongoing exploration.

The shipwreck has been the focus of several commercial surveys and salvage operations over the years. While the State has a policy of monitoring any activity on the wreck, it has also been active in carrying out its own surveys of the wreck site. INFOMAR (the **IN**tegrated Mapping **FO**r the Sustainable Development of Ireland's **MAR**ine Resource), a joint research programme between the Geological Survey Ireland and the Marine Institute, has recently been mapping and identifying shipwrecks in Ireland's territorial waters and on the Continental Shelf. Since 2002 a number of surveys have been carried out on the site of the *Lusitania*, originally under the Irish National Seabed Survey mapping programme and subsequently through INFOMAR. In 2009 more detailed imagery was acquired of the *Lusitania*, using the first of INFOMAR's shallow water survey fleet, the RV *Keary*, and spectacular results began to emerge of the wreck remains on the seabed. Evidence for distinct impact scars, the extent of the debris field and the current condition of the collapsed superstructure are all clearly visible in the images produced by the INFOMAR survey. In 2013 and again in 2014, INFOMAR carried out further detailed surveys of the wreck site, acquiring imagery that continues to

enlighten us on the nature and extent of the remains on the seabed while also providing us with a tangible link to the wreck and its loss over 100 years ago. This information will also help to inform a strategy for the future management and protection of the site in relation to which the National Monuments Service has a key role.

We are in the era of commemorations, including the centenary of the sinking of the *Lusitania,* which was remembered in 2015. This publication draws on a multitude of available sources on the ship and the wreck, including those that have explored theories on the ship and its sinking – Simpson (1972), Ballard (1995) and O'Sullivan (1998 & 2014) for example. Primary source material has been researched, such as contemporary newspaper accounts, the subsequent inquiries and original illustrations and photographic material as well as information from more recent sources published to coincide with the commemoration of the sinking. More recent publications on the wreck are bringing fresh insights and new visual perspectives to the ship and its story, with Eric Sauder's work *The Unseen Lusitania* (2015) perhaps being the most striking. Others too, like Erik Larson's *Dead Wake* (2015) present a more narrative account of the ship and its sinking. The current publication is not meant to be a rehashing of previously published material but rather looks to highlight recent survey work on the wreck and put it in its historical context. While it presents an overview of the ship and its sinking from an historical perspective, it also looks for the first time at the archaeological and technological methodologies that can be applied to the investigation and preservation of this significant shipwreck site.

Presented within the context of a wider management and protection brief for the wreck and its artefacts, the need to apply best national and international practice to any investigation of the wreck site in the future is clearly demonstrated. A synopsis of the statutory protections applicable to the wreck is also presented while the legal background is given in order to clarify the steps taken to protect the wreck to date and to explain the processes that, hopefully, will best serve to manage and preserve the wreck and its artefacts.

This publication contains sections designed to address different aspects of the ship, its history, its loss and the continuing story since it sank. The construction of this great liner is outlined in detail, as are its achievements as the fastest ship in existence at that time. Using results from seabed mapping imagery to support the text, the events leading to its loss and the historical context of the *Lusitania* within the wider events of World War 1 (WWI) and the First Battle of the Atlantic are re-examined. The human tragedy of the loss of the ship is highlighted, the nationalities of the individuals on board discussed as well as the loss of life and the impact of this across many nations. Salvage work undertaken on the site in the intervening years since its loss is synopsised and detail from the more recent archaeologically informed investigation of the wreck site is also included. The archaeological investigation of deepwater shipwrecks is explored, with international examples drawn on. This discussion promotes the application of both national and international best practice and is supported by observations on deep-sea technology that now allow for the proper archaeological investigation of deeply submerged historic wreck sites similar to that of the *Lusitania*. INFOMAR's ongoing seabed mapping programme provides important current imagery of the wreck site and the results are analysed as part of this discussion. Closely linked to such work on deepwater wrecks is the study of the deterioration processes, not least corrosion, with scientific analysis of the structural integrity of these once great ships following many decades on the seabed. Consideration of these processes to inform management and protection strategies is essential. This includes accepting that in some cases, particularly with deepwater wrecks, the inevitability of deterioration over time needs to be recognised and, as natural forces take over, preservation *in situ* is something that cannot be guaranteed.

It is these same natural forces that are now acting on these sites and establishing them as living wrecks, where nature has taken hold and where the marine ecosystem is acting on and being enriched by the growth of the marine organisms which colonise these sites. The potential for research focussed on this aspect is explored for the *Lusitania*, looking at it as a natural and important habitat in its own right.

The publication closes by providing a summary of the chief commemorative events that took place along the southern coast of Cork in May 2015. Central to this was the main commemorative ceremony hosted by the Port of Cork in Cobh, and the commemorative speech delivered by President Michael D. Higgins. Published here for the first time is the full list of all those interred in the three mass grave sites in Old Church Cemetery in Cobh, a catalogue of names that hauntingly illustrates the human tragedy that forms a large part of the story of the *Lusitania*.

There is no doubt that the *Lusitania* was one of the most beautiful liners ever built; its size, speed and opulence ensured that it made maritime history during its heyday crossing the Atlantic. The events and mystery surrounding its loss and wider events relating to WWI, including the great loss of life on board, have equally guaranteed that its story has remained in the hearts and minds of the public ever since. But the story of the *Lusitania* goes beyond its own story as a ship. Recognising the mystery of the great liner and its sinking there is a need to protect this historic wreck in its own right – as an underwater archaeological site of international significance. What follows is an illustrated account of both the ship and the wreck that weds history, archaeology and deep-sea technology to present the past, present and likely future story of the *Lusitania*.

"As the liner settled deeper in the water, the efforts of passengers and crew became more frantic. Panic and tumult were everywhere as excited men and terrified women ran shouting around the decks. Lost children cried shrilly as officers and seamen rushed among the frantic passengers, shouting orders."

R.M.S. "LUSITANIA",
AT LANDING STAGE,
LIVERPOOL.

The Ship

Building the Great Ship

The RMS *Lusitania*, with nine passenger decks, was the largest ship in the world when built and measured over 239m long with a 10m draught. Constructed of high tensile steel plates, held together with triple rows of rivets, it had a double-bottom and a thermo-tank ventilation system that used steam-driven heat exchangers to control the temperature on board. The 31,550-ton steamship was propelled by four giant steam-turbine engines generating 76,000 horsepower and enabling the liner to travel at speeds of 25 knots and, on occasion, faster. This was the first time a merchant ship of this size had been fitted out with steam-turbine engines rather than the usual reciprocating pistons. Other technological advancements included incorporating high tensile steel plating into the hull and locating its most important equipment below the waterline, to protect it from shellfire in case of hostilities. Another innovation was the electric controls for steering, detecting fire and closing the 175 watertight compartments.

In every way, the *Lusitania* broke records and new ground. It was the fastest, the biggest, the grandest and the most famous ship of its time – a true giant of the seas. The *Lusitania's* sister ship the *Mauretania*, completed shortly afterwards, was of equal size. This equally majestic liner began to perform just as well as her sister on crossings of the Atlantic, the *Lusitania* generally winning out on the westbound, Blue Riband, Atlantic crossings until 1909 when the *Mauretania* set a record average speed of 26.6 knots, which stood for 20 years. Both liners were considered the pride of the Cunard line.

Opposite: The *Lusitania* alongside the landing stage at Liverpool. (Ian Lawler Collection)

Rivalry between shipping companies during the first decade of the twentieth century was intense, with major steamship companies from different countries competing to have the largest, most luxurious, modern and fastest ships on the seas. In many respects this competition mirrored the imperial ambitions of the major seagoing nations. The Blue Riband, the unofficial award for fastest westbound liner crossing of the Atlantic, was the ultimate and most sought-after prize in this regard and was a matter of national pride for the competing countries. Several shipping companies vied for the honour, not least the rival lines of White Star, Cunard, Hamburg-America Line and the Norddeutscher Lloyd Line. In the year 1898, the German 14,000-ton liner *Kaiser Wilhelm der Grosse* held the Blue Riband, while the *Deutschland* also held the record for the fastest eastbound crossing. In 1902, the White Star Line was in negotiations with the American company, International Mercantile Marine (IMM), to agree a deal that would see the British company come under the control of the IMM. This would have provided White Star access to far greater financial backing and opportunities and would have given the company the edge in the transatlantic service. On the other hand, Cunard, the pride of British shipping, had not built a new transatlantic liner for nearly a decade and was slowly losing its hold on paying passengers who wished to cross the Atlantic to or from the United States.

The White Star Line was seeking to dominate transatlantic trade and planned to build four new liners. One, the RMS *Olympic*, had already been built and was in service, while plans for the others were well advanced – including the most famous of all, RMS *Titanic*. Cunard felt vulnerable in the face of this challenge and its founding director and chairman,

One of four low pressure turbines under construction in John Brown & Company's yard, Clydebank, Scotland. (Imperial War Museum)

George Burns, Lord Inverclyde, wrote to the British Government seeking financial support to help with a new building programme (Sauder 2015, 10–11). Cunard received assistance on foot of this and it was noted at the time that this was perhaps one of the most important agreements to have been made between a private company and a government – an early and initially successful example of public-private partnership. As part of this

agreement, provision was also made for 12 revolving gun mounts for 6-inch guns, should they be needed as armed merchant cruisers or troopships in time of war. The ship had to be built to comply with various requirements, not least those laid down by Lloyd's, the London-based corporate insurance body. In accordance with Lloyd's Act of 1871 and subsequent Acts of Parliament, Lloyd's stipulated certain requirements pertaining to ship construction that were necessary for compliance with insurance needs. The ship also needed to comply with Admiralty recommendations as a transport and armed cruiser (*ibid.*; Osborne *et al.* 2007).

Right: Pre-launch view of *Lusitania* at the shipyard in the Clyde, Scotland. (Ian Lawler Collection)

Launch of the *Lusitania* as viewed from the port bow side. (Courtesy of the Imperial War Museum)

The sheer scale of the four bronze propellers form an impressive view at the stern of the *Lusitania* as she was about to be launched in June 1906. (Ian Lawler Collection)

Postcard produced in 1908 comparing the huge size of the newly built Cunarders, the *Lusitania* and *Mauretania* with the White City Stadium, London. The stadium was built for the Franco-British Exhibition and used for the Olympic Games in 1908. (Ian Lawler Collection)

John Brown & Company of Clydebank, Glasgow, won the tender to build the first of the two new liners and by 1903 plans were submitted to the Cunard board for consideration (Warren 1986). On 17th August 1904, the steel keel of the hull was laid and construction on the new liner commenced. Originally designed with three funnels, this was quickly changed to four. That the *Lusitania* was built for speed is evidenced by the installation of Parson's steam turbines, which embodied the latest technology, the use of four giant propellors and the location of the main propulsion and auxiliary machinery in nine different watertight compartments (*ibid.*, 15–16, 29–31). The name of the liner was not decided until February 1906, whereupon *Lusitania* and her sister ship the *Mauretania* were named.

Opposite: The bow of the *Lusitania* pictured in dry dock. (Ian Lawler Collection)

A Sight to Behold

Lusitania was officially christened and launched on 7th June 1906. The towering yet sleek design of the liner was to earn it the nickname 'Greyhound of the Seas' and in front of a large crowd waiting on the quayside at Clydebank, the *Lusitania* finally slid into the water at 12.30pm (O'Sullivan 2014, 60). It took nearly 1,000 workers over a year to fit out the liner and it was so large when completed that the channel of the River Clyde had to be deepened and widened to enable it to proceed safely to the open sea. The total cost of building the *Lusitania* was £1,651,870 16*s* 1*d* and when finished it was insured for £1,250,000. A few days before the *Lusitania* set out on its maiden voyage to New York, on 3rd September 1907, visitors were allowed on board. The sheer size of the vessel awed the public, and over 10,000 people

FIRST CLASS LIBRARY, R.M.S. LUSITANIA.

This postcard shows the *Lusitania's* first-class library, which could be used by passengers to amuse themselves on the long transatlantic voyages. (Ian Lawler Collection)

paid to take a guided tour of the ship. All monies collected in this way by Cunard were given to charity. Such was the opulence and grandeur of the interior that one visitor remarked: "If ever a ship deserves to be called a floating palace, the *Lusitania* does" (Sauder 2015, 14, 19).

Internal Splendour

The liner required another year of fitting out at the Tail of the Bank on the Clyde before its sea trials could commence. The ship was fitted out to the highest specifications with first-class accommodation in the neo-classical style of the eighteenth century. The second and third-class accommodation was also of a relatively high standard reflecting the commercial value of the large number of third-class passengers making the emigrant journey to America. Irish passengers were among those travelling in all three sections. Wealthy businessmen, diplomats, royalty, famous people and other élite made up the first-class passengers. Second class was reserved for professionals

and middle-class travellers who made up the bulk of the passengers on board. Third class was inevitably reserved for those less well off or emigrants seeking a better life elsewhere. However, third class in the *Lusitania* was more luxurious than in any previous liner and provided more facilities and better living quarters than had been provided on any previous ship. That being said, and though the issues with vibrations when under full steam were addressed, tremors were still felt at third-class level throughout the sailing life of *Lusitania*.

The overall interior design was contracted to James Miller, a young, talented, Perthshire architect. His dedication to detail ensured that no expense was spared in sculpting the interior into spaces of opulence and style, reflecting the renewed confidence of Cunard in its position as a premier shipping company. First-class accommodation oozed luxury and the main lounge, taking just one example of many stately rooms, had a barrel-vaulted ceiling, sub-divided into 12 stained-glass windows, depicting the 12 months of the year (O'Sullivan 2014, 59). These windows circled the

The passenger liner was equipped with the most up-to-date and comfortable accommodation for first-class passengers, as illustrated in this postcard of the *Lusitania*'s elegantly decorated lounge. (Ian Lawler Collection)

The Verandah Café located near the stern of the vessel for first-class passengers. (Ian Lawler Collection)

LUSITANIA
WALTZ

(Cunard S.S. Lusitania, 45,000 Tons. Length 790 Feet.)

Composed by

EZRA READ.

London:
LONDON MUSIC PUBLISHING STORES LTD. 17ᴬ, LONDON ST. E.C.

760†

Publishers of Ezra Read's EASY Pianoforte Tutor.

AUSTRALIA: E.W. COLE, MELBOURNE.
PRINTED IN ENGLAND.

POPULAR PIANO PIECES:- SPARKLING DIAMONDS; CORNFLOWERS; MIMOSA;
COTTON BLOSSOMS; SUNSET; SWEET PEAS; Composed by Leona Lacoste, these are exceptionally
pretty pieces of moderate difficulty, *Price 1/6 each.*

The *Lusitania* embarking passengers and cargo at Liverpool. (Ian Lawler Collection)

room above equally ornate plasterwork, the greater part of which was designed by the famous company of Bromsgrove Guild; cornices of sea nymphs and shells painted in ivory were illuminated at night time by bulbs hidden behind stained-glass panels. Corinthian style pilasters adorned veneered walls of French mahogany and a jade green carpet with yellow floral design provided a contrast to please the eye. Fourteen marble fireplaces, flanked by Corinthian columns were topped by decorated enameled panels depicting 'The Glory of Sunrise' and 'The Conquest of the Sea'. Another fireplace depicted 'The Music of the Sea and of the Wind' and all combined to provide a sight to behold for both passengers and crew alike (King & Wilson 2015, 101–102).

Opposite: Cover page of the musical score composed by Ezra Read to be played on board the RMS *Lusitania*. (Ian Lawler Collection)

Second class also had exclusive design elements. Smoking rooms for the male passengers and furniture taken from the first class of earlier Cunarders was reinstated in the second-class lounges. Mahogany panelling bedecked the pantry area and decorative plaster graced the ceilings, while tiled floors provided smooth surfaces for those wishing to perambulate after dinner. Third class, though more austere, was surprisingly comfortable. Designed to accommodate large numbers of travellers, with, for example, a dining room capable of sitting 332 diners at any given time, space was sufficient and generally the third-class voyage was comfortable and pleasant during the five-day crossings. The crew too was afforded the highest standard of equipment to work with and the bridge fittings were state-of-the-art for the time. The officers' rooms were also fitted out to a high standard, and were equivalent to that of second-class passengers.

The Lusitania (Cunard Line) New York Harbor. Length 790 Ft. Breadth 88 Ft. 68,000 Horse Powe

The newly built *Lusitania* pictured at night in the Hudson River against New York's lit up sky line. (Ian Lawler Collection)

Passengers pictured on board the *Lusitania* in New York Harbour in 1913 after returning from a baseball trip to Europe. Three collapsible lifeboats can be seen stacked on top of each other on Boat Deck A. (US Library of Congress)

Maiden Voyage and Record-breaking Crossings

The *Lusitania* underwent several sea trials during July and August of 1907, which were reported to have gone relatively well except for a major issue concerning vibrations experienced in the stern of the ship while at full speed. Revised specifications and works were required to address the problem but the vibration issue was never fully resolved. Further sea trials included the liner's first venture into the Atlantic, a 3,000-mile-long weekend cruise with a number of select paying guests circumnavigating Ireland in an anticlockwise direction, which departed from Gourock in Scotland and returned via the Irish Sea to the River Mersey docks in Liverpool. Members of the public were also given several opportunities to visit the ship while it was moored in the Clyde and Liverpool during the sea trials. Thousands marvelled at the majesty, splendour and size of the vessel. Once final adjustments had been made and the sea trials had successfully been completed, the *Lusitania* left the Clyde. It was delivered to Cunard in Liverpool on 27th August 1907, in preparation for her maiden voyage the following week.

On Saturday 7th September 1907, the *Lusitania* departed Liverpool with 2,300 passengers and crew on board and steamed down the Irish Sea stopping at Queenstown (Cobh) to take on mail and passengers before crossing the Atlantic to New York in five days and 54 minutes. Its arrival at the Cunard Pier 54 in New York was a major event: the ship received a rapturous welcome and was hailed as the finest ship in the world. Many thousands visited the liner during the short period it was docked in New York including the celebrated author Mark Twain who commented: "I'll have to tell Noah all about this when I meet him" (Lloyd's List 21st September 1907, 16).

Painting of the RMS *Lusitania* at anchor off Roche's Point, Cork. (Courtesy of Brian Cleare)

Reports received that the *Lusitania* had not in fact outstripped the *Deutschland* and the *Kaiser Wilhelm II* (sister ship to *Kaiser Wilhelm der Grosse*) on its maiden voyage and was therefore unable to reclaim the Blue Riband, were a source of great satisfaction in German shipping circles. The renowned German shipping magnate and owner of the Hamburg-America Line (HAPAG), Albert Ballin, put forward the view at the time that the new ships of the Cunard Line could not be classified strictly as merchant steamers as a result of financial support from the Admiralty and were therefore not eligible for the Blue Riband. This was a somewhat hypocritical view perhaps, given that these and many other HAPAG and Norddeutscher Lloyd (NDL) ships had also been constructed as potential armed merchant cruisers with German government support through their Reichpost contracts with the German Imperial Postal Service.

It did not, in fact, take long for the *Lusitania* to begin to break records for fastest Atlantic crossings. During its second voyage homeward from New York to Liverpool in October 1907, it reclaimed the record from the *Deutschland,* crossing in four days, 19 hours and 52 minutes. Later that month during a westbound voyage the *Lusitania* also reclaimed the Blue Riband for both Cunard and Britain, beating the *Kaiser Wihelm II* by crossing in four days, 22 hours and 53 minutes. Newspapers of the time proclaimed the achievement as follows: "The New Cunarder *Lusitania* on Friday of last week completed her second voyage to New York and broke all records for speed"; and again "On her maiden voyage the *Lusitania* beat all previous best land-to-land records and she has now beaten her own by 5 hours 2 minutes" (*Weekly Irish Times*, 19th October 1907). With the *Lusitania's* newly launched sister ship, the RMS *Mauretania* claiming the Blue Riband later that year, it was stated in Lloyd's List that "The year 1907 will stand out as that in which Great Britain recovered the blue ribbon of the Atlantic. The advent of the *Lusitania* and the *Mauretania* has, indeed, been one of the events of the century" (Lloyd's List 31st December 1907).

A Successful Career

The liner continued to draw massive media attention during its first few months of service, and on one particular voyage in November 1907, it was reported to be the "richest treasure ship which has ever sailed within recent times from an English port" after carrying a half-million pounds worth of gold sovereigns, dollars and bars to New York (Lloyd's List 4th November 1907, 8). The *Lusitania's* sailing career was not without event, even in its early days, and on one occasion a voyage had to be cancelled due to an incident in Liverpool. In April 1908, when leaving the port on its voyage to New York, the *Lusitania* struck the dock wall and damaged one of its propellers. The contemporary account stated that the liner struck the dock wall "damaging one of the protecting pontoons. The pontoon then impinged on the blades of one propeller, snipping the tips of one, two, or more. Divers examined the damage under water, and it was decided to dry-dock the vessel for the purpose of having new propellers fitted" (Lloyd's List 2nd April 1908). The new four-blade propeller design had previously been fitted to the *Lusitania's* sister, the *Mauretania*, and had been found to improve the vibrations that plagued the stern accommodation.

In 1909, *Lusitania* took part in the 300th anniversary of Henry Hudson's trip up the Hudson River. By 1910, with the addition of the Cunarder *Aquitania* – commanded at that point by *Lusitania's* future captain, William Turner – the three ships, *Lusitania*, *Mauretania* and *Aquitania* ensured that on any given week, Cunard had at least one great liner on the North Atlantic route. *Lusitania* completed 91 successful round-trip transatlantic voyages before the outbreak of the Great War in 1914 (www.rmslusitania.info).

The Loss

The Lusitania and the Naval Conflict in Irish Waters

James Lyttleton, *Roy Stokes* and *Karl Brady*

Historians and the State, in previous decades, have largely ignored the impact of the Great War on Irish society. This was due in no small part to the nationalist ethos of the newly independent Irish State, as well as the fraught political environment both during and after the conflict, with the Easter Rising of 1916, the War of Independence and the subsequent Civil War overshadowing Ireland's involvement in that global conflict. In more recent years, however, there has been a growing realisation and acceptance of the country's role in the war effort. When war broke out in August 1914, Ireland was part of the British Empire, and over 200,000 Irishmen enlisted for service in the British,

Following the sinking of the *Lusitania* anti-German sentiments ran high as serious attacks on German nationals and on German-owned businesses led to riots in Liverpool, London and Manchester. This photo shows an angry mob attacking a German-owned shop in London. (Courtesy of the Imperial War Museum)

Early in the war Germany accused England of illegally flying the flag of neutral countries on their merchant ships in an attempt to prevent them from being attacked by German U-boats. (Ian Lawler Collection)

The 15,801-ton White Star liner SS *Arabic* of Liverpool under steam. Torpedoed in August 1915 without warning by the *U-24*, it sank some 45 miles south of the Old Head of Kinsale with the loss of 44 lives. (Painting by Brian Cleare)

Canadian, Australian and American armies. Irish divisions and regiments fought in a number of important campaigns including Gallipoli, Ypres, Passchendale and the Somme. While much of the conflict took place on land, control of the high seas was critical and the Royal Navy and the Kaiserliche Marine (Imperial German Navy) sought dominance over one another in the North Sea, Atlantic Ocean and beyond. There was a prolonged naval engagement spanning 1914–1918 that has since become known as the 'First Battle of the Atlantic'. The war at sea initially involved a German submarine campaign directed against individual vessels of the British Grand Fleet. The first successful submarine attack in the war occurred on 5th September 1914 when *U-21* torpedoed the Royal Navy light-cruiser HMS *Pathfinder* with the loss of 259 British crewmen. With its deadly utility proven, the submarine was to become

a dangerous and often invisible enemy for the remainder of the war.

The strategic location of Ireland, sitting astride the maritime trade routes that linked Britain with its global empire, meant that Irish coastal waters attracted the attention of German war planners. In an effort to disrupt British trade, the Germans launched a deadly submarine campaign against merchant shipping, resulting in the waters to the north and south of Ireland becoming, in effect, 'killing lanes'. The relative safety felt by Allied maritime vessels in the broad expanse of the Atlantic Ocean was lost as soon as they entered the narrowing approaches off the coast of Ireland and the submarine threat resulted in the loss of at least 1,000 vessels (including those flying neutral flags) in Irish waters during the Great War.

In response to such attacks Britain sought to restrict German access to international maritime trade by

A rare photo of the sinking of a vessel by a U-boat. It shows the Allan liner RMS *Hesperian*, sunk by the *U-20* in September 1915, southwest of Fastnet Rock. A lifeboat with the remaining crew and passengers can be seen fleeing from the sinking ship; 33 lives were lost. (Ian Lawler Collection)

implementing a naval blockade, with the Royal Navy successfully confining German naval and merchant fleets to the Baltic and North Seas. German submarines (the U-boats, *Unterseeboot*), however, continued to maraud the waters between Ireland and Britain disrupting Ireland's supply of food and war materials for the British war effort. Even within sight of home, merchant crewmen had to run the gauntlet of the U-boats with their deck guns and torpedoes, as well as risk hitting one of the many mines that had been laid by the Kaiserliche Marine submarines and ships at harbour approaches. Crossing the Irish Sea between Dublin and Holyhead was fraught with danger for crews and passengers who voyaged under constant threat of sinking.

In September 1914, three capital ships, the HMS *Cressy*, *Hogue* and *Aboukir*, were sunk off the Hook of Holland by a German submarine with the loss of nearly 1,500 men. This resulted in the Royal Navy's Grand Fleet being moved to safer waters off the northern and western coasts of Britain and Ireland, to Scapa Flow, an enclosed deepwater harbour in the Orkney Islands, and to Lough Swilly in County Donegal, a long, enclosed, well-protected haven.

A British mark II tank of the 1st Tank Brigade photographed on the ruined streets of Arras, France during the battle of Arras which took place in April and May 1917. The photo, taken by Lieutenant Ernest Brooks, shows that the loss of the *Lusitania* was still in the mind of the military and public at large at the time as illustrated by christening the tank *Lusitania*. (Courtesy of the Imperial War Museum)

One of several German propaganda postcards produced in 1917 celebrating the sinking of high numbers of Allied ships by German U-boats. This particular card celebrates the sinking of 702,000 tons of Allied shipping during December 1917. (Ian Lawler Collection)

Distance, however, provided no significant protection as the German Navy laid mines off the Irish coast. The first sinking in Irish waters took place on 26th October 1914 when the SS *Manchester Commerce* struck a mine off the coast of County Donegal which had been laid by a German armed merchant cruiser, the NDL liner *Berlin*, masquerading as the British HMS *Calabrian*. Two days later, another mine claimed the only Royal Navy capital battleship sunk in the entire war, the HMS *Audacious*. On 13th January 1915, an armed merchant cruiser, the *Viknor*, formerly the *Viking* of the Polytechnic Cruising Company, was sunk 35km north of Tory Island, County Donegal after having struck another mine. There were no survivors of this sinking and many bodies of the 294 on board were washed ashore on the north coast of Ireland. The ship was part of the 10th Cruiser Squadron of armed merchant cruisers that had been enforcing the naval blockade against Germany.

With a stalemate on the Western Front, the Kaiserliche Marine launched an unrestricted submarine campaign in February 1915. U-boats openly roamed British and Irish waters, sinking ships – the most famous of these losses was the RMS *Lusitania*. The international outcry over this incident together with the sinking of the *Arabic*, 80km south of the Old Head of Kinsale (44 lives lost), and of the *Hesperian*, 137km south-west of Fastnet Rock (32 lives lost), had the effect of forcing the Kaiserliche Marine to restrict its attacks on merchant or neutral shipping from September 1915, for fear of bringing America into the war.

The naval facilities at Cobh (then known as Queenstown) became the centre for anti-submarine operations under the command of Admiral Lewis Bayly. By the end of 1916, the fleet at Cobh comprised 15 Q-ships (armed merchant vessels with concealed weapons designed to lure submarines into making surface attacks), 12 sloops, 23 armed steam trawlers, nine drifters, four armed steam yachts, 12 motor launches and four old torpedo boats. Cobh became the hub of Allied naval activity in Ireland (Chatterton

1943). The New Year of 1916, though, saw further attacks. The German submarine *U-80* laid mines on the approach to the naval base at Lough Swilly. One of the many vessels to call into this base was the former White Star liner, the *Laurentic*, now commissioned as an armed merchant cruiser. On 24th January it left Liverpool to transport £5 million in gold bars to the Canadian port of Halifax. The gold which was carried in secret, was payment to Canada and the United States for provision of arms and munitions for the war effort. The following day the liner called into Lough Swilly to avoid submarine attacks in daylight and to allow some naval personnel to disembark. At dusk the *Laurentic* made its way back into open waters, only to strike one or two of the mines that had been laid by *U-80*. The vessel sank in 45 minutes, taking most of the crew and the valuable gold cargo with her. Given that a large quantity of gold bullion was lying on the Donegal seabed, the Royal Navy duly salvaged the

The City of Cork Steam Packet Company steamship, the SS *Inniscarra*, pictured taking cargo on board at Fishguard, Wales. The steamship was torpedoed by the *U-86* and sank approximately 10 miles southeast of Ballycotton shortly after leaving Fishguard for Cork in May 1918. Twenty-eight of the crew died. The SS *Inniscarra* was one of six City of Cork Steam Packet Company steamships torpedoed and sunk during the war with the total resultant loss of 119 lives. (Ian Lawler Collection)

US Navy divers with a torpedo which they recovered from the *UC-42* in 1918. The *UC-42* sank while attempting to lay mines near the entrance to Cork Harbour in September 1917 with the loss of all 27 crew on board. (NH82756: Courtesy of Naval History and Heritage Command)

The USS *L-2* at anchor in Bantry Bay, County Cork in July 1918. The *L-2* had just recently returned to base in Bantry after completing a patrol near Fastnet Lighthouse. While on the patrol, an unidentified German U-boat surfaced in front of the US submarine but before the *L-2* could attack, the German U-boat exploded and sank with the loss of all on board.
(NH51121: Courtesy of Naval History and Heritage Command)

wreck over a number of years afterwards to recover the gold bars; by 1924, when official salvage operations ceased, 3,186 of the 3,211 bars were recovered (Wreck Inventory of Ireland Database (WIID)).

In February 1917 the German Navy declared a second 'unrestricted U-boat campaign'. There were heavy losses in Irish waters during the spring of 1917, followed by a short-lived reduction in U-boat activity before an increase again for the remainder of the year. The Kaiserliche Marine calculated that if its submarines could sink 600,000 tons of Allied merchant shipping per month, then Britain would be starved of vital overseas supplies and would be forced to surrender. In February, 540,000 tons of shipping was sunk, followed by 603,000 tons in March. Given the trend, it was estimated by British naval authorities that Britain would have to surrender before the end of November 1917. German U-boat commanders like Otto Steinbrinck in *UC-65* and Johannes Lohs in *UC-75* were hugely successful in attacking Allied shipping in Irish waters. Steinbrinck sank 18 vessels between 24th and 28th March while Lohs sank 115 vessels during 10 months of service before he lost his life in November 1917 when his submarine was torpedoed by

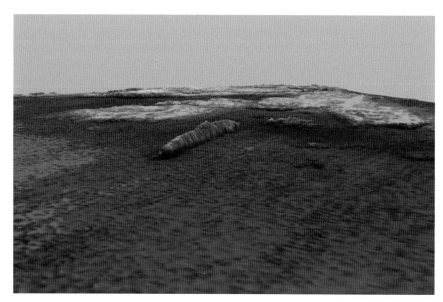

The *UC-42* was lost during an attempt to lay mines across the mouth of Cork Harbour in September 1917 when a mine accidentally detonated, resulting in the loss of the submarine and all 27 crew on board. Located 5km southeast of Roches Point, the *UC-42* is orientated NW/SE on the seabed and is relatively intact. It measures 36m x 5m and lies at a depth of 26m. It was originally discovered during a 2010 survey by INFOMAR; the RV *Keary* resurveyed the site in 2012.

A rare photo of a vessel being torpedoed by a U-boat during WWI. The *Falaba* was a 4,086-ton steamship owned by the Elder Line. It was en route from Liverpool to Sierra Leone with 151 passengers, 96 crew and a cargo valued at £50,000 on board. On 28th March, 1915 approximately 43km south of the Saltees the steamship was stopped by the *U-28* which issued an order to abandon ship. Before this operation could be completed, however, the U-boat fired a single torpedo which resulted in the vessel rapidly sinking and the loss of 104 lives. (Ian Lawler Collection)

a British submarine. In May, the British authorities introduced the convoy system with merchant vessels grouped together for their protection rather than sailing in isolation. This proved quite successful and in the three months following the system's introduction, of the nearly 9,000 vessels that sailed in these convoys in the Atlantic and North Sea, only 27 were lost to submarine attacks. In contrast, 356 vessels sailing independently were sunk (Grant 1964; Massie 2004).

Due partially to persistent attacks on American shipping in the Atlantic Ocean, the United States finally entered the war in April 1917. The Royal Navy's fleet in Cobh was strengthened by the addition of US naval vessels. Berehaven in Bantry Bay was also to become an important base for both the American and British navies. Now American destroyers, cruisers, submarines and submarine chasers were patrolling the southern approaches to Ireland and escorting transatlantic convoys to safe havens. A notable success for the US Navy was the capture and sinking of a

The City of Cork Steam Packet Company steamship, the SS *Innisfallen*, pictured docked in Bristol, England. The steamship was torpedoed and sunk en route from Liverpool to Cork by the *UB-64* in May 1918, approximately 24 miles east-southeast of Lambay Island. Ten lives were lost but the captain and 23 others were saved. (Ian Lawler Collection)

Crew members on board the *U-89* while in harbour in Germany. The *U-89* sank off the coast of Donegal in February 1918 after unwittingly surfacing in the path of the HMS *Roxburgh*, which duly rammed it, nearly splitting the submarine in two with the loss of all 43 submariners. (Ian Lawler Collection)

German submarine, *U-58*, by the USS *Fanning* and USS *Nicholson* off the Cork coastline in November 1917. Forced to the surface, the *U-58* was scuttled by its crew before the Americans could take over the vessel, but the incident was considered a major success, as it was the first sinking of an enemy submarine in US naval history. The German authorities were under no

illusion that, given enough time, the entry of this industrial giant would ultimately decide the outcome of the war. It was now imperative that the movement of American personnel and materials into the Western Front be hindered by a major spring offensive by the German army in 1918. U-boats continued to attack shipping on the western approaches to Ireland in order

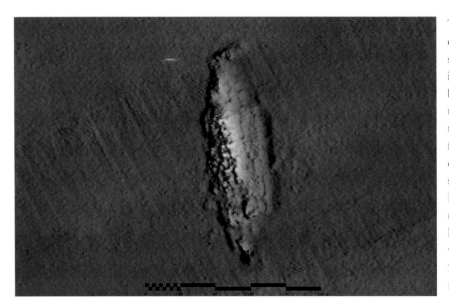

The *Justicia* is clearly discernible against the stony seabed in the multibeam imagery. The 12 giant Scotch boilers, standing over 8m above the seabed, run in pairs along the length of the wreck, followed by the two enormous eight-cylinder, triple-expansion steam engines. A slight scour has developed at its S end (lower section), exposing the largely intact bow. The wreck was surveyed by the RV *Keary* in 2012 as part of INFOMAR's mapping programme.

to inhibit the build-up of American military strength. Early attempts were made at 'wolf pack' tactics (*rudeltaktick*) with concerted attacks made upon troop and munitions carriers, but such efforts were in vain. By the spring of 1918, the United States was also using ports on the west coast of France, with thousands of American troops being disembarked to relieve the over-stretched British and French armies (Massie 2004).

Attacks continued off the Irish coastline; a troopship, the liner *Justicia*, which was just as large as the *Lusitania*, en route from Belfast to America, was attacked by three submarines, the *U-54*, *UB-64* and *UB-124*. It was a prolonged attack that began on 19th July and continued until the vessel was sunk the following day. The *Justicia* was one of many troop transports attacked and sunk in the northern approaches to Britain and Ireland in 1918 in an effort by German submarine crews to improve the chances of victory for their comrades-in-arms on the Western Front. In October 1918 the RMS *Leinster*, a mail packet boat that regularly plied the Irish Sea, was attacked and sunk by *UB-123*, just 12 miles out from Dun Laoghaire en route to Holyhead. The submarine fired three torpedoes, one passing across the *Leinster's* bow, the second striking her on the port side and the third on her starboard side after it had turned in an attempt to return to harbour. Over 500 lives were lost in the sinking, the majority of whom were military personnel. It is one of the cruel ironies of war that *UB-123* and her crew did not survive much longer themselves as their submarine was sunk in a minefield on the return journey to Germany.

A few weeks later, in November, an armistice was agreed and the subsequent truce brought the Great War to a close, a war that saw unprecedented death and destruction, including the loss of Irish vessels and many lives close to home. The experience of those who worked for the City of Cork Steam Packet Company was not atypical for Irish crewmen at the time. Six of that company's cargo steamers – the *Inniscarra*, the *Innisfallen*, the *Ardmore*, the *Lismore*, the *Kenmare* and the *Bandon* – were attacked without warning by German submarines. In all, 119 lives were lost during these attacks. Among other merchant vessels that were sunk was the *W.M. Barkley*, a

Guinness-owned vessel torpedoed without warning off the coast of Dublin in October 1917 with the loss of four lives, including the ship's master. The SS *Adela* was attacked and sunk en route from Dublin to Liverpool with the loss of 24 lives. Fishing vessels were not excluded from attack either; the *St Michan* and the *Geraldine* were sunk off Lambay Island in March 1918 with all lives lost. And it was not all one way; the Kaiserliche Marine also suffered losses – 15 of the 178 U-boats sunk during the Great War were lost in Irish waters. A number of these submarines have now been located and surveyed, including the *U-89* and *UB-124* off the coast of Donegal and the *UC-42* and *U-58* off Cork.

Loss of the Great Liner

With the outbreak of WWI in 1914 plans to use the *Lusitania* as a naval vessel were shelved due to its enormous coal consumption. It was observed at the time that the liner used up to 70 tons of coal per hour while at full power, far in excess of what was economically acceptable to the Admiralty at the time. This also meant that the ship could not spend enough time at sea to make an effective patrol. During the initial months of the hostilities the *Lusitania* avoided major incident, but following the commencement of unrestricted submarine warfare in February 1915, the waters around Britain and Ireland were declared a war zone and immediately became more dangerous to naval, mercantile, fishing and passenger vessels. The number of ships and boats attacked and sunk without warning began to rise significantly and even neutral vessels that entered these waters were at risk.

Prior to the *Lusitania* completing its 101st round trip from New York to Liverpool on Saturday 1st May 1915, the German Embassy in Washington published a notice in 40 American newspapers advising intending passengers that the waters around Britain and Ireland were a war zone. Newspapers of the time tell of the indignation felt by passengers at the insertion of what was perceived as German propaganda material into newspapers in advance of the sailing, warning citizens not to make the voyage (*The Times* 8th May 1915, 9). There is no record,

Painting by Brian Cleare giving a dramatic impression of t

g of the *Lusitania*. (Courtesy of B. Cleare and C. Kelleher)

however, of anyone cancelling their tickets as a result, with American passengers believing instead in their Government's warning to Germany that it would be held to "strict accountability" for any damage to American life or property (*ibid.*). A notice was issued at the same time by the German Embassy stating that ships flying the British flag were deemed by them to be "liable to destruction" and that travellers sailing in these waters "do so at their own risk" (Imperial German Embassy, 22nd April 1915). The warning, however, was largely ignored by Cunard and the travelling passengers while *Lusitania's* captain, William J. Turner was of the opinion that the *Lusitania* could outrun any threats the U-boats posed.

The *Lusitania* departed New York to huge media interest as a result of the German warning. While fast liners like the *Lusitania* routinely carried munitions to Britain, in the opinion of the German government the *Lusitania* was carrying contraband. This was in the form of cargo that neutrals were forbidden to supply to those engaged in war. It is still a controversial issue but, under regulations governing American and international shipping at the time, it was permissible for the *Lusitania* to be carrying what were termed small arms ammunition, non-explosive in bulk. In this regard, the *Lusitania* carried 1,248 cases of 3.3-inch shrapnel shells (unfilled), 4,927 cases of rifle bullets with around 1,000 cartridges per case, 3,240 percussion fuses for 6-inch shells and 46 tons of aluminium powder. Furthermore, on 30th April, shortly before sailing, 70 passengers and 200 tons of cargo were transferred from the *Queen Margaret* to the *Lusitania*, and part of the transferred cargo was ammunition. This is borne out in the archives of the Remington Arms Company which include a letter that refers to the loading of 2,000 cases of small arms ammunition on to the *Queen Margaret*; attached to this letter was a Cunard receipt for 2,000 cases of .303 ammunition, with the name *Queen Margaret* cancelled and *Lusitania* written across it (Moore 2012, 62). Again, this has been a source of controversy over the years, but it was apparently common practice for a ship to embark on an abbreviated manifest and to supply a full one after leaving port. In the case of the *Lusitania*, the complete manifest listed all the arms it

Captain Turner (1856–1933) on the flying bridge of the RMS *Aquitania* during an earlier command in 1914. Captain Turner is in his Commander's uniform of the Royal Naval Reserve. Although Turner was criticised in some quarters for his role in the loss of the *Lusitania*, he was awarded an OBE in 1918. (National Maritime Museum, Greenwich)

was legally carrying and this information was in the public domain shortly after the sinking. One thing that cannot be disputed, however, is that these arms were destined for use in the British war effort (Simpson 1983, 104–109).

Although carrying arms and decked out to carry guns, the *Lusitania* should not have been targeted without advance warning and the passengers and crew should have been allowed to leave the ship safely. The so-called 'cruiser rules' governing this practice stemmed from an attempt to regulate naval warfare from the second half of the nineteenth century, with the Declaration of Paris in 1856 and later the Hague Convention (1899 and 1907). Both stated that passenger ships or merchant vessels could not be targeted until those on board were safely allowed to leave or were taken to safety in advance of any military

U-20 in dock (front row, second from left) alongside the *U-19*, *U-21* and *U-22* in Germany in 1914/1915. (US Library of Congress)

Painting by Claus Bergen of the liner's last moments before it sank beneath the waves. The German artist produced many depictions of naval warfare during both world wars and was employed as Marine Painter for Kaiser Wilhelm II during WWI. (Ian Lawler Collection)

Postcard issued after the sinking of the liner showing the women and children boarding the lifeboats in a calm and controlled fashion. However, the reality of evacuation was much different due to the speed at which the liner sank. For example, many of the port side lifeboats could not be launched due to the ship listing to the starboard, and many other lifeboats overturned while being lowered. (Ian Lawler Collection)

action being carried out (Salgado & Russo 2014, 24). The actions of the captain and crew of *U-20* therefore appear to have contravened or deliberately ignored this international maritime and naval convention.

The first four days of the *Lusitania's* last voyage were relatively uneventful, but on nearing the Irish coast, the captain of the ill-fated liner, William Turner, received warnings that there was recent submarine activity in the area. His actions in response to the warnings are still disputed, but it would seem that he reduced the speed of the vessel from 21 knots (its maximum speed at the time) to 18 knots in the hope of catching the full tide on the way into Liverpool and to avoid hanging off the Liverpool coast in what he may have thought would have been a position more vulnerable to U-boat attack. Captain Turner also maintained a straight course rather than employing the zigzag manoeuvre recommended to help avoid attack by U-boats. On the afternoon of 7th May the liner was detected, passing the Old Head of Kinsale, and

attacked by *U-20* under the command of *Kapitänleutnant* Walther Schwieger. Eyewitness statements, given at the inquiry held in June 1915 by Captain Turner and the lookouts in the crow's nest and forecastle head have the torpedo striking midships on the starboard side, under the bridge or just aft of it. (https://www.titanicinquiry.org/Lusitania/) Another explosion followed, most likely in the boiler room or coal storage areas in the forward part of the ship. The cause of this second explosion has remained a mystery and a subject of controversy to this very day.

The Sinking and Rescue Efforts

The *Lusitania* sank in 18 minutes. Accounts describing the event are harrowing and one can only imagine what must have gone through the minds of those on board in the moments when the torpedo struck and the time thereafter when it became clear that the great liner was going down. Patrick O'Sullivan, in his book,

Another in a series of postcards issued after the sinking of the *Lusitania* showing lifeboats pulling away from the sinking liner attempting to rescue survivors in the water. (Ian Lawler Collection)

provides a graphic overview of these final minutes in a way that gives a real sense of the tragedy and horror of the events.

> "As the liner settled deeper in the water, the efforts of passengers and crew became more frantic. Panic and tumult were everywhere as excited men and terrified women ran shouting around the decks. Lost children cried shrilly as officers and seamen rushed among the frantic passengers, shouting orders. Women clung desperately to their husbands while others knelt and prayed. The screams of frightened men and women in the water added to the terror of those still on board." (2014, 122–123).

Survivor accounts similarly can help us comprehend these final moments and many of these are tellingly reproduced by Molony (2004) in his book on the Irish on board. One in particular is especially distressing. Told by Florence O'Sullivan, a third-class passenger from Kilgarvan, County Kerry, who was returning home with his wife after a number of years living in the United States, the account is both extensive and graphic. Florence recounts that he "saw it happen". He stated: "I saw the ripples in the water – it was like a fish. It came from the landward side. Then I heard a crash, something like the sound of glass broken with a hammer. When I found things were wrong I rushed down to the cabin for lifebelts and when I returned, after an absence of ten or eleven minutes, I found the deck awash."

Mr O'Sullivan continues to describe the way the ship began to rapidly incline, with children being forced to clamber up the railings (Molony 2004, 66–67). Julia O'Sullivan, Florence's wife, similarly leaves a dramatic and very poignant account of those who were not so lucky. "It was simply awful to hear the hundreds of drowning men, women and children shouting and crying for help." Separated from Florence, Julia was eventually brought safely to Kinsale; she had spent four hours in the water clinging to a raft and was unconscious when picked up. Florence similarly tells of the wails of those drowning: "The cries and

No. 8.—THE DOOMED "LUSITANIA" : How the Irish Rescuers Hurried to the Scene of the Tragedy.

Striking illustration published in *The Sphere* newspaper a week after the tragedy of the sinking of the liner showing the subsequent rescue attempts by boats from the surrounding areas. (Ian Lawler Collection)

'The Track of the *Lusitania*' as titled by its painter, William Lionel Wyllie. The graphic painting shows the trail of debris, destruction and death left after the sinking of the great liner. (National Maritime Museum, Greenwich)

Postcard showing rescue ships arriving at the scene of the lost liner. (Ian Lawler Collection)

lamentations of the women and children and the shouting of men were something dreadful." He too spent several hours in the water, where he drifted about, frequently encountering "other hapless victims, and striking up against dead bodies" (*ibid.*, 68).

Both Florence and his wife survived but hundreds of others were not so fortunate, and many drowned as a consequence of the difficulty in launching the 22 standard and 26 collapsible lifeboats. This is supported in Florence O'Sullivan's account, where he states that many of the lifeboats overturned during launch, others were broken against the side of the liner as it listed to starboard and he witnessed one splitting in two when it hit the water, with all on board thrown out. He did not consider the lifeboats safe and chose instead to jump into the water and cling to flotsam (*ibid.*). Perhaps it was this that ensured both he and his wife survived.

Trawlers and tugs in the area quickly came to the aid of the sinking vessel, as did local fishing boats. The word of the tragedy quickly spread with the *Lusitania's* wireless operator sending out frantic Morse Code messages and seeking assistance. Land's End Wireless Station, at 2.20pm noted: "Distress call made by

steamer *Lusitania* at 2.13pm, as follows: 'Come at once, big list, position 10 miles south Kinsale'". Another picked up by Brow Head Wireless Station in south-west Cork, at 3.20pm recorded: "Steamer *Lusitania* in distress 10 miles south of Kinsale at 2.15pm". At Queenstown the radio records from 2.58pm detail: "Reported that steamer *Lusitania* sank at 2.33pm south-west of Kinsale" and "Steamer *Lusitania*: Admiral commanding all available vessels at this port to render assistance" (Lloyd's List Saturday 8th May 1915, 31, 480). The latter command was from Vice-Admiral Coke of Queenstown which mobilised the varied fleets of trawlers, tugs and torpedo boats. The nearest vessel to the *Lusitania* was in fact a Manx fishing lugger, the *Wanderer*, and its skipper, Captain Ball and his crew had witnessed the explosions. The fishing boat headed straight to the sinking liner and rescued over 150 passengers from the lifeboats. Heading for Cobh, the *Wanderer* towed two more lifeboats full of survivors as there was no more space on board. Other vessels in the area included the *Dan O'Connell* which rescued 18 survivors and recovered up to 60 bodies. It had, only two days earlier,

Four of the lifeboats which were successfully launched from the *Lusitania* pictured at Cobh as printed in *The Sphere* newspaper a week after the tragedy. (Ian Lawler Collection)

Photo printed in *The Sphere* newspaper a week after the tragedy showing the fishing vessels the *Elizabeth* and the *Wanderer* at Kinsale which were both involved in rescuing 190 people from the sinking ship. (Ian Lawler Collection)

Edward White of Arklow, skipper of the *Elizabeth* which was involved in the rescue of survivors from the sinking ship. (Ian Lawler Collection)

rescued survivors from the schooner *Earl of Lathom*, which, ironically, had also been sunk by the *U-20* off the Old Head of Kinsale (O'Sullivan 2014, 126–128). Other local vessels were tasked with recovering the dead, and the steamship *Heron* along with two trawlers, in one day alone, brought over 100 victims into Cobh, most of them women. The tug *Polzee* arrived with 16 bodies, including three babies (*ibid.*, 128–129).

Over the course of the next four to five hours, rescue boats rowed or steamed out of Kinsale, Cobh and the surrounding areas. The first rowed vessel on the scene, the lifeboat *Keria Gwilt*, came from Courtmacsherry. The station at that time was located at Barry's Point, west of the present day village, and it was from there that the brave men on the lifeboat rowed the 24km to the tragic scene. The sloop HMS *Bluebell* rescued many, including Captain Turner himself, and in all, over 760 passengers and crew were rescued and survived. These fortunate survivors made up less than half of the complement of passengers and crew on board the *Lusitania*, comprising individuals from all walks of life and from many nations around the world.

What Caused a Second Explosion?

At the time, the possibility that there was a second explosion, potentially caused by a second torpedo, fuelled the propaganda machine and served to heighten the outrage at the sinking. Theories continue to abound and over the years numerous hypotheses have been discussed, debated, discredited or dismissed. Suggestions range from ignition of aluminium powder to exploding ammunition; boiler explosion or steam line rupture are equally mooted. Others have proposed a coal dust explosion or the setting off of a possible pipe bomb by German spies on board – perhaps one of the three stowaways? Others again debate if there was in fact a second torpedo or if the first and second explosion were both caused by the first and only

torpedo striking the ship (www.rmslusitania.info). Indeed a detailed discussion was published by Wood, Smith and Hayns (2002, 188) that considered all options. They concluded that the second explosion came from within the ship itself, suggesting that a boiler explosion was the most likely cause, but one that was not an isolated event. Instead it formed part of "separate and unconnected occurrences that amalgamated into one second explosion" and that led to the catastrophic events that sank the liner so quickly. In effect, a "series of power-plant based explosions and major (explosive-like) structural failures took place over a period of several minutes after the torpedo detonated" which corroborates the testimonies of several surviving passengers who recounted the timescales between when the torpedo struck and the "second explosion" taking place (ibid.).

What can be said with certainty is that this debate will continue as the location of the second explosion

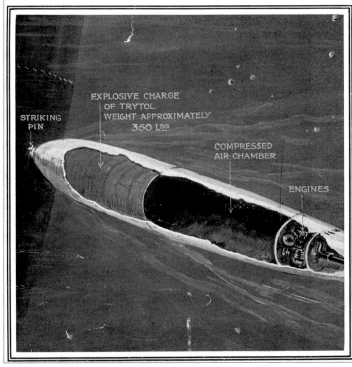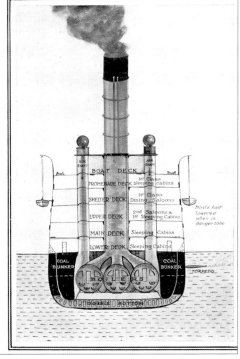

Illustration of the type of highly charged torpedo which would have been fired by the *U-20* causing the *Lusitania* to sink in 18 minutes (*The Sphere*, 15th May 1915). (Ian Lawler Collection)

Schematic illustration showing the estimated damage caused by the highly charged torpedo fired from the *U-20* (*The Sphere*, 15th May 1915). (Ian Lawler Collection)

will not readily reveal itself. The wreck lies on its starboard side, with the bow section, where the torpedo is known to have struck, side down on the seabed; thus direct visual evidence for the impact is not currently available. Conclusive evidence might never be forthcoming but informed discussion and measured debate have maintained a focus on the possible causes for the second explosion and rapid sinking. Presented here are the considered views of a former Irish Naval Ordnance officer and explosives expert, who ponders again the possible scenarios that might have caused the second or indeed 'a secondary' explosion and puts forward his hypothesis to explain events.

The Debate Continues

by Commandant (Ret.) Peter Daly, former OIC Naval Ordnance, Irish Naval Service

"I was about three decks down in the ballroom when all of a sudden there was a terrific bang. All the lights went out. I made my way up to the top deck as fast as I could and when I finally arrived she was listing over to the starboard side, pretty steep. I managed to get bundled into number 13 lifeboat, and I was lowered away down to the water's edge. The thing I noticed was all the water rushing in through the portholes – it was such a lovely day, you know – all the water rushing in, every porthole open. Of course that made her sink much quicker than she would have done, I think. When we were a little distance away from the ship there must have been a terrific explosion down below, because you could see all the cinders and everything and debris getting blown out of the funnels. And of course her stern end came right up out of the water and then she went straight down, clean as a whistle."

Survivor, bellboy William Burrows,
aged 15 years; 10th May 1915
(Molony 2004, 110)

Many survivors, when questioned afterwards, reported hearing two explosions following the torpedo strike. The captain of *U-20* subsequently insisted, and his logs show, that only one torpedo was fired. When the torpedo hit the ship it was always likely that it would trigger a secondary explosion in the ship's hold. The exact cause of such an explosion is still very much a matter of debate as the ship was known to have been carrying substantial quantities of .303 bullets, unfilled shrapnel shells and aluminium powder to supply the British war effort. None of this material was considered to be potentially explosive or a danger to passengers and was not considered to be contraband when traded by a neutral power. However, this is disputed by many and the motivation behind some recent research initiatives was to try and see if evidence could be found to show that the second explosion was a result of gun cotton or some other explosive substance having been ignited by the impact of the torpedo. Mr F. Gregg Bemis Jnr, owner of the wreck of the *Lusitania*, has promoted much of this research. Other recent dives on the wreck, particularly by Cork diver Patrick Glavin and his team, have identified cases of .303 cartridges, but noted no evidence of an explosion in the storage area containing them.

From a purely historical viewpoint it does not really matter what caused the 'secondary explosion'. As we step down the 'why staircase' we come to the root cause. A torpedo struck the ship shortly after 2.10pm on Friday 7th May 1915, in fine clear weather off the Old Head of Kinsale. It was struck without warning and sank in under 20 minutes. Much play has been made then and since of the fact that the *Lusitania* was carrying munitions. The facts are that it was known before it sailed that munitions were being carried, and that was not unusual as the *Lusitania* was a British ship. What was unusual was that it was primarily a passenger ship. From a propaganda point of view the fact that passengers (including American citizens) were effectively being used as 'human shields' was something to be concealed on one side and exploited on the other.

It is a fact that there was a subsequent blast, or more accurately a 'secondary explosion'. The *Lusitania* was not the first passenger ship to be torpedoed nor the first to sink quickly having been struck by a torpedo, but it is worth considering what might have been the cause of the secondary explosion. It is

Opposite: The sinking of the *Lusitania* was used to promote recruitment to the British armed forces in Ireland and Britain, and as propaganda to help push American opinion towards joining the war effort against Germany. The over dramatised form of the poster shows the effects of a large explosion taking place on the *Lusitania* as it sinks beneath the waves. (US Library of Congress)

necessary to look at the evidence available and the first key piece of evidence is the magnitude and nature of the secondary explosion; this should provide guidance as to where to look for the cause. Nowhere in any of the reports has it been suggested that the secondary explosion was significantly greater than the first, though witness accounts tell of seeing its effects more clearly. Much of this may be because many of those witnesses were in the water by that time and able to view the sinking liner. There is an important technical difference between high and low explosives – high explosives detonate and low explosives merely explode. The mechanism of detonation and the energy levels are quite different. The munitions listed on the so-called second manifest, i.e. small arms ammunition fuses and shrapnel shells, cannot have been the cause of the secondary explosion because they are not capable of a mass explosion. There were other items on the second manifest, described as foodstuffs such as butter and bacon, about which there has been speculation that they could have been high explosives. It is possible that it was these explosives and not the listed munitions that were the cause. This is of course conceivable but not very likely. If those items were in reality high explosives then the secondary explosion would almost certainly have been akin to a direct hit on a ship's magazine – a spectacular and obvious detonation.

There are two other more prosaic but more likely causes: a coal dust explosion and a boiler explosion. *Lusitania* was a steam ship with coal-fired boilers. It was funded and designed at the outset to be converted into an armed merchant cruiser in wartime. The coal bunkers were positioned so they could be filled from the outside and accessed by the stokers inside to feed the furnaces. In effect they formed part of the protection of the ship from gunfire. As the bunkers were emptied, significant quantities of coal dust remained. From the impact of the torpedo a dust cloud could have formed and, if a suitable spark or source of ignition were available, an explosion could have taken place. The most likely cause of the secondary explosion, however, was that a boiler exploded as a result of ingress by tons of cold seawater causing rupture of a heated boiler. Such an explosion on a steam ship was a common enough event, and descriptions by survivors of these events, of being showered with coal dust and other debris, supports that premise. Certainly the account by bellboy William Burrows suggests a boiler explosion for the cause of the second explosion.

At this historical remove it is telling that theories and investigations into the possible cause of a secondary explosion that led to the rapid and catastrophic sinking of the *Lusitania* are still in play 100 years after the event.

Passengers & Crew

Nationalities of Passengers and Crew

It is difficult to trace accurately the totality of nationalities represented by those who were on board the liner but what can be said with certainty is that its loss touched a multitude of nations across the world so that the story of the RMS *Lusitania* remains a global one.

Among those listed in the crew and passenger lists are not only many individuals from the USA, Britain and Ireland but also from Canada, Russia, Norway, Persia, Cuba, France, The Netherlands, Italy, Greece, Switzerland, Brazil and Belgium. While this reflects the diverse range of nationalities recorded as being on the ship, it does not accurately reflect all nationalities that were actually on the ship. Many of those listed as Russian, for example, were in fact Polish or Finnish, many Canadians, Australians and Irish living in the UK were listed as 'British', while many first-generation Irish-Americans were listed as American. There is therefore more research to be done to elucidate the true nationalities of all who were on board the *Lusitania* when it sank.

Little is known of the three stowaways apart from the fact that they were all German. Apprehended shortly after the *Lusitania* had left New York on its last voyage, the three were interrogated by Detective-Inspector William Pierpoint, with Adolph Pederson acting as translator for the three. They were imprisoned below deck, most probably in third-class level and were locked away when the ship sank. Their identities remain a mystery (www.rmslusitania.info.).

The excellent *Lusitania Resource* website provides a comprehensive list of all passengers and crew on board as well as statistics pertaining to them

(www.rmslusitania.info/people/statistics/). In total there were 1,960 on board the *Lusitania* when it sank. These comprised:

- 290 first-class passengers, of whom 113 survived and 177 died.
- 601 second-class passengers, of whom 229 survived and 372 died.
- 373 third-class passengers, of whom 134 survived and 239 died.
- 69 deck crew, of whom 37 survived and 32 died.
- 313 engineering crew, of whom 112 survived and 201 died.
- 306 victualling/service crew, of whom 139 survived and 167 died.
- 5 band members, of whom 3 survived, 2 died.
- 3 German stowaways, in third class, all 3 died.

In total, 767 were rescued; 1,193 died at the wreck site (including the three stowaways) and if we include the four survivors who died shortly after being rescued, then in total, 1,197 died as a direct result of the sinking of the ship.

The Irish on Board the Lusitania

Of the 1,960 passengers and crew on board the *Lusitania*, 90 were listed as Irish, comprising men, women and children. Most were lost when the liner went down, with many of the bodies recovered and interred in the Old Church Cemetery in Cobh. The most comprehensive study of the Irish connection with the *Lusitania* is Senan Molony's *Lusitania: An Irish Tragedy* (2004). Molony rightly states that if first-generation Irish from Britain and the United States were included, the numbers of those on board connected directly to Ireland would grow incrementally, and indeed many of the crew, most especially those employed as firemen and trimmers, were Irish emigrants resident in port towns like Liverpool who sought employment in the boiler rooms of passenger ships such as the *Lusitania*. Similarly, many were emigrants returning from the United States on holidays or after a few years working there. Emigration from Ireland across the Irish Sea or Atlantic Ocean grew from the mid-nineteenth century, and with the advent of faster crossing times, such travel became more accessible and return journeys equally so. Passenger travel increased as a result, with the faster crossing times opening up the opportunity to return home more regularly or to join relatives who had already migrated across the seas.

In keeping with the convention of the time, the *Lusitania* was divided into three classes. Irish passengers were among those travelling in all three sections. As well as passengers, the *Lusitania* had over 690 crew, including the officers commanding the ship, medical staff, nurses and doctors. The ship housed a 24-bed hospital on the shelter deck, including the nursery and an isolation ward in the event of infectious diseases, all located in the stern of the ship. One of the ship's surgeons was Irishman Dr Joseph Garry from Kildysart, County Clare who was only 25 years of age when he drowned; Dr Ralph Mecredy of Bray, County Wicklow, who was travelling as a second-class passenger, was saved and his story told below is quite remarkable (Molony 2004, 57, 80). The body of *Lusitania's* second surgeon, Dr James McDermott, originally from Cork but then living in Liverpool, was recovered and interred in Cobh's Old Church Cemetery. One sad story of many relates to Dr McDermott treating third-class passenger Annie Kelly, from Mountbellew in County Galway, during the outward journey. She was making the trip from Cobh to New York to join her boyfriend William Murphy who had emigrated earlier. A routine medical examination by McDermott led to the discovery that the 19-year-old suffered from a heart defect. As a result she was detained in Ellis Island, to be deported back to Ireland, the US emigration authority having ruled that she was not fully fit to work. Her return passage was

A handbill produced by Sir Hugh Lane's brother in the aftermath of the sinking of the *Lusitania* in the hope that the body could be identified should it have been recovered. (National Library of Ireland)

Headstone erected in memory of William Henry Winters by his wife in Mount Jerome Cemetery in Dublin. (Photo Karl Brady)

Some of the survivors of the sinking on shore in Cobh shortly after the disaster. Among them is Francis Toner (with moustache and without coat) who survived three shipwrecking events, the *Titanic*, the *Empress of Ireland* and the *Lusitania*. (*Irish Examiner*)

Commonwealth War Graves Commission headstone of James F. McDermott, surgeon on board the *Lusitania* when it sank. Unfortunately for the surgeon who was originally from Cork, he had temporarily replaced the ship's regular surgeon who had just taken ill prior to the *Lusitania*'s fateful and last voyage. (Photo Connie Kelleher)

booked on the *Lusitania*. Both Annie Kelly and James McDermott lost their lives when the ship was torpedoed (Molony 2004, 41, 86–87).

Catering and room service staff, clerical and administrative staff and those men located in the bowels of the ship supplying the boilers with up to 70 tons of coal per day, made up the remaining crew. Irish men and women were equally well represented among all of the crew but the actual figures for Irish on board the ship are difficult to determine fully as the passenger manifest lists most as being British. Certainly those in the boiler rooms were predominantly Irish, including

firemen, trimmers, stokers and greasers though many may have then been living in Liverpool. Molony (2004, 23–96) again provides a gripping overview of those Irish he has identified, with background stories and details of their survival or loss, subsequent lives or burial following the sinking of the liner. Individuals such as fireman W. Barry, 26 years old from Dublin or Patrick Brown, trimmer, 24 years of age from Sligo, were drowned. Sarah (Sadie) Hale, another victim, from Ballymena, County Antrim was 29 years old and was one of Cunard's clerical staff. Her job required frequent travel on board Cunard's ships from Liverpool to New York and she was on board the liner as the ship's typist. Her informal letter to her mother some months before the sinking outlining how she wanted her estate dealt with in the event of her death set a precedent in maritime law as it was accepted as being as legally binding as a will considering she was technically a mariner and at sea when she wrote it (*ibid.*, 81–83).

Sir Hugh Lane, whose body was never recovered, is perhaps among the most well known of the Irish on board and was one of the passengers in first class. Others enjoying the comfort of first-class travel included William Hunter from Mountpleasant Square, Ranelagh, Dublin who was Cunard's culinary consultant and Michael Byrne, a special deputy sheriff

Alfred Vanderbilt pictured on the Cunard Pier, New York in 1913. Vanderbilt, a sportsman and New York millionaire, was one of the more famous victims of the disaster. He was noted as assisting many on board the liner as it sank but did not survive himself and his body was never recovered. Alfred's sister, Gertude Vanderbilt Whitney partially funded the erection of the *Lusitania* monument in Cobh, County Cork. (US Library of Congress)

in New York and a native of Paulstown, Kilkenny, who was on his way to Ireland to visit family and friends.

Fr Basil Maturin from Grangegorman, Dublin, 67 years of age, was lost but his body was subsequently recovered by a patrol boat some eight miles south-west of the Fastnet Rock and brought ashore in Crookhaven. Fr Maturin's body was transported to Cobh and then onto London where he was interred following a Requiem Mass in Westminster Cathedral

(*ibid.*, 22–24, 49–50). While each story of loss or survival that has been recorded has its own particular resonance, one or two verge on the unbelievable. The calm recollections of Dr Ralph Mecredy are extraordinary as he recounts his deliberations walking the ship from bow to stern wondering what end to jump from in order to maximise his chances of being picked up and not being dragged under. He eventually found a rope ladder which trailed off into a metal wire

Some of the survivors of the sinking on shore in Cobh wearing clothes and blankets they had been given by the local community. (*Irish Examiner*)

THE WELL-KNOWN PEOPLE WHO WERE TRAVELLING ON HER.

he passengers are going aboard along the gangways which lead from Railway Station.

Lady Mackworth, daughter of Mr. D. A. Thomas, and wife of Sir H. Mackworth, Bart.

Nearing completion. She was launched at Clydebank nine years ago, and made her maiden voyage about twelve months later.

Mr. D. A. Thomas, the Welsh coal magnate, who was on board with his daughter.

Sir Hugh Lane, the famous expert, and director of National Gallery of Ireland. Has done much to revive Irish art.

Mr. Charles Frohman, the famous theatrical manager, who produced Barrie's plays. He has an international reputation. He was on board the vessel.

The Old Head of Kinsale, Ireland, off which the vessel went down.

Pictures in the *Daily Mirror* (8th May 1915) of some of the better known passengers who were on board the *Lusitania* when it sank including Hugh Lane, American theatre manager Charles Frohman, Welsh coal magnate D.A. Thomas and his daughter Lady Mackworth. (National Monuments Service, Department of Culture, Heritage and the Gaeltacht)

One of the victims of the *Lusitania* covered by the American flag being brought to the morgue in Cobh. (US Library of Congress)

which he slid down, burning his hands but grateful for the healing properties of the cold water as he was pushed under by a stoker coming down the rope after him. While surrounded by scenes of panic he seemed to move through it all in a state of absolute calmness, eventually pulling himself on board a lifeboat without being invited and observing the infamous second explosion from a safe distance! (*ibid.*, 57–60). The story of Dublin man Francis Toner, one of the firemen on board, is also extraordinary and not just for surviving the sinking of the *Lusitania*. As his tale emerged it turned out that he was also a fireman on board the *Titanic* when it sank on its maiden voyage in 1912 and subsequently on the *Empress of Ireland* that sank in the St Lawrence River in Canada in 1914, with a comparable loss of life to that of the *Lusitania* (*ibid.*, 91–92).

Sadly, the remains of most of those lost were never recovered. The bodies recovered from the sea immediately after the sinking were brought ashore at Cobh while many more were washed ashore around the coast over the coming weeks. Such was the number of those washed up on the coast that groups of body-finders were established to check the shorelines regularly. The remains of 169 individuals, including men, women and children were interred in the three mass graves in the Old Church Cemetery in Cobh, while other victims were interred in burial grounds all around Ireland. While some of these could be identified, many were unidentifiable after being washed up on some lonely shore days or even weeks after the sinking. Graveyards in Cork, Kerry, Clare, Dublin and Galway, including the Aran Islands, and Mayo contain the remains of many victims of the sinking, either interred in family plots, having been brought there by relatives or interred locally after being washed ashore.

Other Nationalities on Board

As outlined above, many individuals representing various nationalities were victims of the sinking. Of those who survived, some first-hand accounts are available. An Italian doctor, Silvio B. de Vescovi, was picked up by the rescue vessel *Westborough*, where Dr de Vescovi proceeded to amputate the injured arm of Owen Slavin. Slavin, from Dundalk, was a trimmer on board and had been injured when the torpedo struck. Dr de Vescovi also administered aid to Lady Allan and some other women who were on board the *Westborough*. Mr Julian de Ayala, the only Cuban listed on board, was the Consul General at Liverpool. He was ill at the time, but managed to get into a lifeboat and was rescued. Russian father of eight, Samuel Abramowitz, who was a successful businessman and regularly made the journey to London and New York

MATT FREEMAN
THE "HERO" OF
THE LUSITANIA

The story of British 19-year old Matthew Freeman, who was a waiter on board the doomed liner, is one of survival. He assisted with the launch of lifeboats following the torpedo strike but hurt his arm in the process. This delayed his exit from the ship and he eventually had to jump from the stern, though it was high out of the water. He struck his head on a floating lifeboat when he hit the water but kept swimming. Another man grabbed him in an attempt to survive, but ended up submerging Freeman. He again surfaced and grabbed a floating deckchair. A doctor, Daniel Moore, urged Freeman to catch onto a barrel, which he did. Eventually they made it to an upturned lifeboat and held on to it while it acted as a raft. Freeman spent nearly one and a half hours in the water until he was finally rescued by the patrol boat *Brock*. In 1955 Matthew Freeman was recorded as living in Miami, Florida. At the time of his rescue, postcards were produced calling him 'the Hero of the *Lusitania*' due to his surviving against so many odds.
(www.rmslusitania.info)
(Ian Lawler Collection)

from his base in France, was well known to members of the crew. Having safely boarded one of the lifeboats, Abramowitz was instrumental in saving several passengers including a newly born baby. On being landed in Queenstown, he subsequently assisted with the recovery of bodies and this left an indelible mark on him for the remainder of his life (www.rmslusitania.info). While many other accounts are available, the similarities in the actions and reactions of survivors are indicative of the commonality of purpose and unity of spirit that surpassed cultural differences to form a universal bond in that moment of crisis. With the sinking of the *Lusitania*, the world was momentarily united in grief and horror at such great loss of life in the cruellest of circumstances.

Truths & Mistruths

Inquiries and Inquests

The international reaction to the sinking of the great liner, along with the sinking of the White Star liner *Arabic*, 80km south of the Old Head of Kinsale, and of the *Hesperian*, 137km south-west of Fastnet Rock, forced the Kaiserliche Marine to restrict its attacks on merchant or neutral shipping by September 1915 and to comply with international Prize Rules. The sinking of the RMS *Lusitania*, however, had been celebrated in Germany and was used by Britain and her allies as a means of exerting pressure on America to enter the war. Two public hearings followed the sinking. One immediately after the sinking was held in Kinsale and chaired by coroner J. J. Horgan and the second one was chaired by Lord Mersey in Westminster, in June 1915. A court hearing to settle the claims of the Cunard Company was also convened by Judge Julius Mayer in New York in 1918.

Following the sinking both victims and survivors were brought into Cobh and Kinsale. The latter town also became the centre of international attention when the first inquest into the deaths was held in the local courthouse. Coroner J. J. Horgan was the driving force behind the inquiry and he arranged several key witnesses, including Captain Turner, to give evidence well before any similar inquiry could be organised in Britain. The fateful verdict of the jury of the inquest at Kinsale was 'Wilful and Wholesale Murder' not only against the German officers and command of the submarine *U-20* but also against the German government and the *Kaiser* himself (Molony 2004, 143). Though looked upon with some disdain in Britain, as a small and somewhat irrelevant undertaking, the inquest in Kinsale served to exonerate Captain Turner from all blame for the sinking. A

Part of the funeral cortège which brought victims of the sinking to the Old Church Cemetery in Cobh for burial on 10th May 1915. (*Irish Examiner*)

similar verdict was also reached by Lord Mersey in the subsequent inquiry despite pressure from Churchill, First Lord of the Admiralty, and the First Sea Lord, Admiral Fisher, to pin the blame on Turner, and have him portrayed as somehow in league with the Germans. The primary motivation for this would seem to have been to deflect any suspicion away from Churchill and the British Admiralty that the protection afforded the *Lusitania* when it entered dangerous waters was anything but adequate. Admiral Fisher,

Burial service at the Old Church Cemetery in Cobh where 170 of the 289 bodies recovered from the *Lusitania* were buried. (*Irish Examiner*)

The bodies being buried in mass graves in Old Church Cemetery, Cobh. (Ian Lawler Collection)

acting
on a report compiled by Captain Richard Webb, based on Turner's debriefing, wrote in the margins of the report: "I feel absolutely certain Turner is a Scoundrel and [has] been bribed. No seaman in his senses would have acted as he did. I hope that Captain Turner will be arrested immediately after the inquiry, whatever the verdict or finding might be". Churchill added the following: "I consider the Admiralty case against the Captain should be pressed before Lord Mersey by a skilful counsel and that Captain Webb should attend as witness, if not employed as an assessor. We should pursue the Captain without check" (Ramsay 2001, 118–120). As Ramsay points out, Captain Webb's report was flimsy and inadequate, compiled only a day after the sinking, was highly subjective and would seem to have been deliberately misleading on some of the important facts, accusing Turner of only travelling at three quarters of the speed he could have and not allowing Turner to explain his actions in the lead up to the sinking. One explanation for Churchill's willingness to go along with the scapegoating of Turner was not to alert the Kriegsmarine that the Admiralty could read their codes. Therefore, by pinning the blame on Turner it would lessen the need to explain the Royal Navy's role and intelligence gathering methods for protecting vessels at sea (*ibid.*, 119–120).

Grave marking a number of "victims of the Lusitania outrage" in St Multose graveyard, Kinsale, including George Craduck and Richard Chamberlain. Recently a plaque commemorating a third victim, that of young Scottish bride Margaret MacKensie Shineman, was also added to the grave site. (Photo Connie Kelleher)

On 15th June 1915, Lord Mersey, Wreck Commissioner for the United Kingdom, convened the UK Board of Trade inquiry into the sinking of the *Lusitania* at the Central Buildings, Westminster. This was the first formal investigation into the sinking and comprised six sittings between 15th and 18th June, 1st July and 17th July. Lord Mersey's inquiry was thorough in that it included investigation of the ship itself and its appurtenances; the voyage and speed of the vessel; the torpedoing and orders given after it struck, and the navigation carried out with respect to the route taken by the *Lusitania*. The investigation placed the blame for the tragedy firmly at the feet of the Germans and exonerated fully both the captain and crew of the *Lusitania:* "The whole blame for the destruction of life in this catastrophe must rest solely with those who plotted and with those who committed the crime" (Peifer 2016, 80–82).

In New York, a separate inquiry also took place in 1918, following the receipt of 67 claims for compensation to the Cunard Company. Presided over by Judge Julius Mayer, a number of witnesses, including British survivors, gave evidence, while statements from others were read out. Captain Turner also appeared and vehemently argued his case, including claiming that sailing in a zigzag motion was not necessary. Mixed accounts of when and where the torpedo hit were heard, with accusations of portholes

having been left open and thereby accelerating the sinking also being made. In his findings, however, Judge Mayer categorically laid the blame squarely on Germany, stating that "the cause of the sinking was the illegal act of the Imperial German Government" (Preston 2002, 366–370).

Lusitania and United States Involvement

"The crew of a fishing yawl found an upturned lifeboat seven miles off Schull yesterday, marked '22A, *Lusitania*, Liverpool', which they brought to Long Island. Pinned beneath were the bodies of four women and two boys." (*The Times* 13th May 1915, 5)

Of the four women, two were American with one identified as a Miss Taylor from Dorchester, Massachusetts. Though accounts vary slightly, it is generally accepted that there were some 159 American passengers travelling on board the *Lusitania* when it sank. Of these a reported 128 drowned. Among the American passengers who lost their lives were some notable and influential people including Alfred Gwynne Vanderbilt, a wealthy sportsman and member of the famous philanthropic family of that name; Mr A. L. Hopkins, president of the Newport News Shipbuilding and Dry Dock Company; famous theatre producer Charles Frohman; American fashion designer Carrie Kennedy and her sister Kathryn Hickson; Anne Shymer, successful chemist and president of the United States Chemical Company and American genealogist and historian Lothrop Withington.

Though some reports have traditionally suggested that the sinking of the *Lusitania* was the catalyst for the United States entering WWI, it was not immediately the case. In the intervening period between the sinking of the liner and US entry into the war in 1917, political pressure and diplomatic dialogue between the national governments involved were complex, protracted and strained. Certainly, anti-German opinion escalated as a result of the sinking but the US president, Woodrow Wilson, was determined to keep the US out of the war as long as he could, viewing it as a European conflict while intent on maintaining US neutrality and ensuring the continuation of trade, mercantile commerce and livelihoods for his citizens at home (Martin 2014, 95). He was also conscious that the British would use it as a powerful weapon in their propaganda war to gain American support for their blockade of the North Atlantic. American support would give Britain the capacity to sustain the blockade and curtail the free movement of shipping in an area that was crucial for German supplies (Preston 2002, 315). The diplomatic pressure mounted, especially with continued and almost immediate loss of other vessels through German submarine warfare. While this gave added strength to the argument being made by those who advocated that the US should enter the war effort, it took almost two more years for this to come about.

In August 1915, just three months after the *Lusitania* was sunk, the White Star liner *Arabic* was torpedoed off the south-west coast of Ireland and 44 lives were lost, including two Americans. Following this, the German Government pledged not to target passenger liners. Despite this pledge, however, in September 1915, the Allan liner RMS *Hesperian* was sunk by a German submarine, south-west of the Fastnet Rock. While the *Hesperian* did not sink immediately, allowing most of the passengers and crew to launch the lifeboats, it was not without a certain added poignancy. The torpedo that struck the ship was fired from the *U-20*, the same submarine that sank the *Lusitania* and under the same commander, *Kapitänleutnant* Walther Schwieger. On board the *Hesperian* were the remains of Mrs Francis Stephens, a victim of the *Lusitania* sinking, which were being transported back to Montreal for burial with her husband (Wreck Inventory of Ireland Database). Furthermore, on 8th November 1915 the Italian passenger steamer, SS *Ancona*, built in 1908 in Belfast, was torpedoed by German submarine *U-38* and sank off the coast of Sardinia with the loss of over 200 lives, including nine Americans. In what became known as the 'Ancona Incident', the US sought sanctions from Germany, who in turn agreed to pay an indemnity and punish the German officer in command of the *U-38*. This never materialised, but Germany did agree once

Opposite: Satirical postcard produced by French artist Emil Dupuis in 1916 entitled '*A L'ombre de la Liberté*' or '*In the Shadow of Liberty*'. The card criticises the hypocrisy of the US for remaining neutral and placing its economic interests first in the aftermath of the sinking of the *Lusitania* and associated loss of Americans lives. (Ian Lawler Collection)

more to refrain from attacking passenger vessels flying neutral flags. Meanwhile Britain continued with its blockade of the North Sea, which was viewed by many, including Germany, as illegal. Not only did this disrupt enemy shipping but it seriously impacted neutral mercantile trade, not least US ships and particularly those American cargo vessels that legitimately entered and left German and Northern European ports on a regular basis. Britain argued that all shipping could pass safely if they agreed to search and inspection, and a series of strategically placed mine fields within the North Sea area allowed British naval patrols to control the area. It was generally believed that in pursuing this course of action, Britain was, in fact, in breach of international maritime law (Martin 2014, 100). While negotiating with Germany at this time, US President Woodrow Wilson was also debating whether America should impose embargoes on Britain because of its blockade in the North Sea (*ibid.*).

In January 1916, the Glen-owned liner, *Glengyle* was sunk in the Mediterranean and the same month the P&O liner *Persia* was lost through submarine action off Malta. Both resulted in the loss of more American lives, including the American consul to Aden, lost when the *Persia* went down. US political commentary became more pointed, with the chairman of the Senate Committee stating "that no excuse can be found for such an action as there were few officers and soldiers aboard the ship" (*The Manchester Guardian* 4th January 1916). The targeting of passenger and mercantile shipping by German submarines continued, however, in 1916, with the sinking of the *Sussex* in the English Channel and the loss of 80 people, including Americans (Martin 2014, 109).

On 26th February 1917 the liner *Laconia* was sunk off the south coast of Ireland, with 26 American lives among those lost. This coincided with the interception of a telegram by British Intelligence, sent by Germany

A l'ombre de la Liberté...   *ÉTATS-UNIS*

In the shadow of Liberty.

THE LUSITANIA TORPED

Cunard's Mammoth Liner That Cost Eight Minutes—1,918 Souls

DASH OF RESCUE SHIPS IN REPLY TO "S.O.S." C

Huns Carry Out Advertised Threat to Murder Neutral Passengers.

WILL UNITED STATES TAKE IT LYING DOWN?

THE LUSITANIA WAS TORPEDOED YESTERDAY BY A GERMAN SUBMARINE.

OUR PIRATE FOES HAVE THUS CARRIED OUT THEIR THREAT OF MURDER AND COMMITTED THE FOULEST OF A LONG SERIES OF MISDEEDS.

THE LUSITANIA HAD ON BOARD 1,918 SOULS—1,253 PASSENGERS AND 665 CREW.

NO NOTICE WAS GIVEN BY THE PIRATES BEFORE THEY TORPEDOED THE LUSITANIA, WHICH SANK IN EIGHT MINUTES.

SHE WAS A VESSEL OF 30,396 TONS AND WAS BUILT IN 1907, COSTING £7,250,000. SHE WAS AN ARMED LINER COMPLYING WITH THE ADMIRALTY REQUIREMENTS

BEYOND THE FACT THAT THE CUNARD COMPANY HAD ASCERTAINED THAT MANY LIVES HAD BEEN SAVED, NO DEFINITE NEWS WAS RECEIVED UP TO A LATE HOUR LAST NIGHT.

THE BOAT WAS FULL OF IMPORTANT AND WEALTHY PEOPLE, AMONG THE BEST-KNOWN BEING MR. ALFRED VANDERBILT, MR. CHARLES FROHMAN AND MR. D. A. THOMAS, THE WELSH COAL MAGNATE.

As soon as the Lusitania's dramatic "S.O.S." of "Come at once, big list," was received every available craft left Queenstown to render aid.

The Lusitania's doom was by then sealed and the rescuing vessels immediately began to search for passengers.

It appears that the Lusitania was noticed to be in difficulties from the signal station at the Old Head of Kinsale at 2.12 p.m. At 2.33 she had completely disappeared.

The London offices of the company receiv the following telegram from Liverpool:—

"Several boats, apparently from Lusitan nine miles south-east Queenstown. Gre steamer proceeding to assist."

SANK IN EIGHT MINUTES

The giant liner, says a Central News Quee town message, was torpedoed off Galley Hea on the other side of Kinsale, at 2.25 p.m., a sank within eight minutes.

She carried a large mail.

A fleet of steamers was immediately d patched from Queenstown to rescue passenge

When the disaster occurred the weather w beautifully fine, with a hot sun and a gen southerly breeze.

Among the rescuing boats sent out is a fle of ten trawlers, one of which had the Quee town lifeboat in tow.

"SOS" CALL SENT OU BY THE DOOMED LINER.

It was in the City—in the heart of the shippi quarter—that the sinking of the huge liner fir became known, and caused intense excitemen

The information was brief but too complet A message posted at Lloyd's yesterday ran :—

"The Admiralty report that the Lusitan was sunk off the Old Head of Kinsale at 2. this afternoon."

The Cunard Company's Liverpool office ceived a message from Land's End saying th

---

1,918 IN DOOMED LINER.

The Cunard Company states that there were 1,918 people on board the Lusitania The total was made up as follows:— Passengers: First-class, 290; second-class, 602; third-class, 361. Crew, 665.

---

the Lusitania sent out wireless messages: "Come at once, big list."

According to another account it is stated th the liner's wireless message, with regard to h list, said: "We are listing 10deg."

Passengers have been saved, but how many

:D BY GERMAN PIRATES

,250,000 Sunk in Board.

┃ MANY LIVES SAVED

USHED TO LEARN FATE OF DEAR ONES.

hetic Scenes at Cunard Of.ices—Man in Tears for Wife.

athetic scenes took place at the London
ces of the Cunard Company in Palmerston
use, Bishopsgate-street, when the news of
Lusitania's fate was announced.

riends and relatives of the passengers began
nce to flock to the offices, and the officials
staff of the company were kept at high pres-
e throughout the night answering anxious
uiries about dear ones on board the lost
sel.

ne woman rushed through the main en-
nce up to the counter in a hysterical condi-
i, and she had to be comfroted by friends
o accompanied her.

ler anxiety concerned the safety of her
ther and sister, who were on the ill-fated
sel. So soon after the disaster, however, no
sfactory information could be given.

o one and all, indeed, the officials made the
ne reply—that all they knew was contained
the Admiralty report.

ne of the most pathetic sights in the offices
s an elderly married pair, with grey hair,
o sat quietly and composedly in a corner.
ey were a clergyman and his wife, waiting
news of their son, who was returning in
Lusitania after a lecture tour in America.

ne American, almost broken with fear and
kiety, said he waited for news of his wife,
o went out to America four weeks ago. "I
iled to her to come back by the Lusitania,"
said, with tears in his eyes, "as she was the
y boat that could get away from the German
marines."

mericans in London could talk of nothing
this new instance of "frightfulness."

t the Savoy Hotel a group of Americans
hered about the news bulletin board dis-
ssing the tragedy.

That settles it," exclaimed a white-haired
zen of the United States. "We've got to
n the Allies now. If President Wilson doesn't
np in our people will push him in."

NAMES OF PASSENGERS.

OFFICIAL NOTICE OF MURDER PLAN.

Huns' Warning Threat to Passengers Not to Sail.

"TO EASE OUR CONSCIENCE."

The officials of the Cunard Line in New York
and all the passengers sailing in the Lusitania
had received indirect notice from the German
Ambassador at Washington that the Lusitania
was in peril, the intimation being that the
German submarines would try to torpedo the
gigantic liner.

The following advertisement appeared in the
New York and other American newspapers a
few days before the Lusitania sailed:—

> **TRAVELLERS** intending to embark for an
> Atlantic voyage are reminded that a state of
> war exists between Germany and her Allies
> and Great Britain and her Allies; that the
> zone of war includes the waters adjacent
> to the British Isles; that, in accordance with
> the formal notice given by the Imperial Ger-
> man Government, vessels flying the flag of
> Great Britain or any of her Allies are liable
> to destruction in those waters; and that
> travellers sailing in the war zone in ships of
> Great Britain or her Allies do so at their own
> risk.
> **IMPERIAL GERMAN EMBASSY,**
> **WASHINGTON, APRIL 22.**

When the saloon passengers boarded the Lusitania most of them were handed a telegram
signed "John Smith" or "John Jones," warning them that they would imperil their lives if
they sailed in the Lusitania. Most of the
passengers paid no attention to the wires.

Mr. Alfred Vanderbilt, member of the famous
New York millionaire house, who lives in London, was a passenger in the Lusitania. He received one of the warning wires, but tore it up
without making any comment.

The telegram which failed to frighten Mr.
Alfred Vanderbilt read: "Have it on definite

PREVIOUS GREAT DISASTERS.

Date.	Ship.	Lives Lost.
May, 1914—	Empress of Ireland	1,012
Oct. 1913—	Volturno	126
April, 1912—	Titanic	1,503
Feb., 1910—	General Chanzy	200
Sept., 1909—	Waratah	211
Nov. 1908—	Taish	

to the Foreign Minister in Mexico, in which Germany stated that it intended to continue its submarine warfare and if required would seek an alliance with Mexico if the US did not remain neutral. More worryingly for the US, Germany suggested to Mexico that an alliance with Japan should also be considered if the US entered the war (*ibid.*, 111). While commentators then and since have cast doubt on the authenticity of this telegram, its alleged content proved to be the breaking point for the US, particularly as such an alliance would be at its own back door. Woodrow Wilson, following unprecedented pressure from his own cabinet, agreed to enter the war on the understanding that he was doing so to ensure the safety and security of Americans at home.

On 6th April 1917 the US officially entered WWI. While its entry was protracted, and at times it had more issues with Britain's blockade of the North Sea than it did with Germany's targeting of neutral vessels, it is unquestionable that it was, somewhat ironically, Germany's successful submarine warfare and U-boat tactics that were the instrument that ultimately led to US entry into the war. Thus, on 4th May 1917 (only two years after the sinking of the *Lusitania*), British Admiral Bayly welcomed the first American destroyers into the harbour at Cobh, County Cork, where they established an officers station, field hospital and Naval Air Station. From then on the presence of US personnel in Irish waters was a significant element of the war effort and left an indelible imprint on the history of Cobh and Cork Harbour (Brunicardi 2012, 107–118).

Propaganda, Political Impact and the Irish Cause

The sinking of the *Lusitania* brought home to the public the true savagery of the twentieth century's 'modern' methods of war in a way that can be compared to the effect of the World Trade Centre attack at the start of the twenty-first century. The

A few months after the sinking of the *Lusitania* the German satirical medallist Karl Goetz produced a medal intended to castigate the British for their disregard for possible civilian casualties in sending the *Lusitania* through a 'war zone'. Unfortunately for Goetz, he took the date of the sinking from an incorrect news report and as a result the medal bears the date 5th May, instead of 7th May. Inevitably, the British acquired a copy and over 300,000 copies were produced, along with a leaflet explaining that this was proof of Germany's intention to sink the *Lusitania*, without any regard for the possible loss of non-combatants' lives. (Ian Lawler Collection)

Lusitania was the second passenger ship to be sunk, following the sinking of the *Falaba* the previous March. In that instance, and in accordance with accepted practice at the time, the U-boat surfaced, ordered the liner to stop and gave those aboard the opportunity to abandon ship. Unfortunately, however, the U-boat commander, fearful that Royal Navy vessels might be approaching, launched the torpedo before everyone could get to the lifeboats, with the consequent loss of 104 lives. The *Lusitania* sinking was so much more shocking for the general public, not only due to the number of casualties but also because the ship was sunk suddenly with no warning. Moreover, in contrast to previous wars, innocent civilians appeared to be fair game.

Stung by the international outcry, in August 1915 the Munich medallist Karl Goetz designed and cast a satirical medal castigating the Allies for allowing passenger vessels transit through a 'war zone'. The text on the reverse of the medallion states: "DER GROSS-DAMPFER *LUSITANIA* DURCH EIN DEUTSCHES TAUCHBOOT VERSENKT 5. MAI 1915". It translates as: "The great steam ship *Lusitania* sunk by a German submarine 5 May 1915" (Dutton 1986). Furthermore, he depicted the *Lusitania* as carrying war materiel. Goetz made a fateful error in the date of the sinking, an error which he ascribed to

Emotive propaganda poster using an image of a mother and child drowning as a result of the sinking of the *Lusitania* (poster produced by Fred Spear in June 1915). Numerous posters, postcards, pamphlets, coins, medals and other paraphernalia were produced by both sides for propaganda purposes and to encourage men to enlist in the army or navy in the aftermath of the sinking. (US Library of Congress)

an erroneous newspaper report, recording the strike as the 5th rather than the 7th of May. Inevitably an example of the medal made its way to the British side where it was seized upon as providing conclusive proof that the Germans had planned to sink the *Lusitania* all along. While Goetz maintained in November 1916 that only 180 of his medals were in existence, hundreds of thousands of replicas were produced on the orders of the Director of Naval Intelligence, Captain Reginald Hall, and distributed around the world each in a presentation box with an explanatory leaflet in English or other European languages. Smaller numbers were also produced in the United States (Burns 2012).

This marked the beginning of a propaganda war in which images of German 'atrocities' such as the *Lusitania*, the Zeppelin bombings and the execution of

the English nurse Edith Cavell for helping British soldiers escape from German-occupied Belgium were deployed to encourage people to support the Allied war effort. The *Lusitania* figured prominently on a number of recruiting posters exhorting men to enlist. What are now termed 'cinderella' stamps were produced and sold to support a variety of war-related causes. Other medallions and tokens were struck, postcards printed and all sold to support the war effort while reminding everyone of the 'barbarity' of the Germans. In the United States even milk bottle tops featured the liner *Lusitania*!

In Ireland too, the sinking of the *Lusitania* fed into a propaganda machine with a dual agenda, and the tragedy had an interesting part to play in national politics thereafter. On the one hand thousands of

Propaganda poster by W.A. Rogers portraying drowned women, men and children in one of the *Lusitania's* lifeboats resting at the bottom of the sea. This is one of numerous posters and cards produced to try to inflame American public opinion against Germany and to encourage recruits to enlist in the army or navy. (US Library of Congress)

Irishmen had joined the Allied forces to fight and die on European battlefields and many had joined up because of the sinking by the Germans of the great liner, reacting to the propaganda posters of *'Remember the Lusitania'* or *'Irishmen Avenge the Lusitania'*. At home, however, the movement for independence from Britain was gaining in intensity in 1915 and by the first anniversary of its sinking the 1916 rebellion had been defeated but Irish politics was to change forever in the aftermath. The British took the opportunity of the sinking to put out propaganda that Germany was attacking Munster and thus Ireland and in this way hoped to garner more support from Irish volunteers for the British war effort (Molony 2004, 11–13).

The postponement of Home Rule for Ireland by the British Government on the outbreak of WWI led to a feeling among nationalists that it would never be implemented. The arming of the unionist Ulster Volunteers in April of 1914 and the nationalist Irish Volunteers in July of the same year highlighted the deep divisions within the country for and against Home Rule. The Irish volunteers were set up in November 1913 in opposition to the Ulster Volunteers to defend Home Rule and "to secure the rights and liberties common to all the people of Ireland" while the Ulster Volunteers, formally established the previous January, threatened to resist the implementation of the Act of Union and the authority of any Dublin Parliament by force of arms. The stage was set for civil war if Home Rule was implemented but its shelving in September 1914 following the outbreak of war saw volunteers from both traditions fighting side by side on the battlefields of Europe. In the meantime certain nationalist sentiment at home turned to Germany as a source for more arms and support. The cause of Irish nationhood was more important than supporting British causes overseas. Propaganda abounded on all sides to encourage support for one cause or the other. While the propaganda coup for the British war effort arising from the sinking of the *Lusitania* was an increase in Irishmen enlisting in the British Army, many nationalist members of the Irish Volunteers who remained at home experienced some hostility from those whose family members were fighting on foreign soil.

In the US, however, the Irish Republican Brotherhood saw Irish participation in the British war effort as further undermining the cause of Irish freedom, and the lack of reporting on the loss of Irish-Americans on board the *Lusitania* fuelled this viewpoint. At times in Ireland, a social war took place with disputes between neighbours sometimes resulting in loss of life. Irish pro-British sympathisers fought pro-German supporters serving only to add to the tragedy of events unfolding during a time of escalating unrest and change (*ibid.*, 16–17). The series of mishaps leading up to and following the landing of Roger Casement in Kerry, resulting in the scuttling of the German gun-running ship, the *Aud*, in April of 1916 outside Cork Harbour, was indicative of the complexities of sentiment at play at that time. The

The first six islanders to be evacuated from the Great Blasket Island (*An Bhlascaoid Mhóir*) on 17th November 1953, one of whom, Seán Ó Guithín, is carrying a prized possession, a deck chair from the *Lusitania*. The deck chair is one of many items from the liner that were washed up on the west coast in the months following the sinking and it is now in the Blasket Centre in Dunquin, County Kerry (*Ionad an Bhlascaoid Mhóir*). Image courtesy of the Irish Examiner Newspaper.

Pictured left to right: Seán 'Sheáisí' Ó Cearna, Pádraig 'Fiogach' Mistéal, Seán Ó Súilleabháin, Seán 'Fílí' Ó Cearna, Seán Ó Guithín, Seán 'Faeilí' Ó Catháin

planned rebellion went ahead on a reduced scale, the executed leaders became martyrs and sparked the more focused and concentrated move for independence which followed the war. Propaganda, as always, played its part and American public opinion was ultimately again at the centre of things when Britain agreed to concede a certain measure of independence to Ireland with the signing of the Treaty in 1921. The complexities of this period and the extraordinary consequences of individual actions are clear to be seen in the story of Captain Raimund Weisbach, the German Commander of the U-boat

that landed Roger Casement in Kerry in his unsuccessful attempt to rendezvous with the *Aud* and land arms for rebellion. Just a year earlier Weisbach was the officer who fired the torpedo that struck the *Lusitania*. The failure to land Casement's arms led to a much more curtailed rebellion that ultimately, perhaps due to that failure, changed the course of Irish history while the torpedo Weisbach fired influenced American public opinion and contributed to America eventually entering the war, in this case changing the course of world history.

"It will be gathered, therefore, that the *Lusitania* Salvage Company of Philadelphia has a very difficult, if not an impossible, task before it, and that in any case the enterprise will require the support of philanthropists or of persons who would not mind what money they lose in the hope of ascertaining all that happened to the torpedoed liner."

SECTION 3

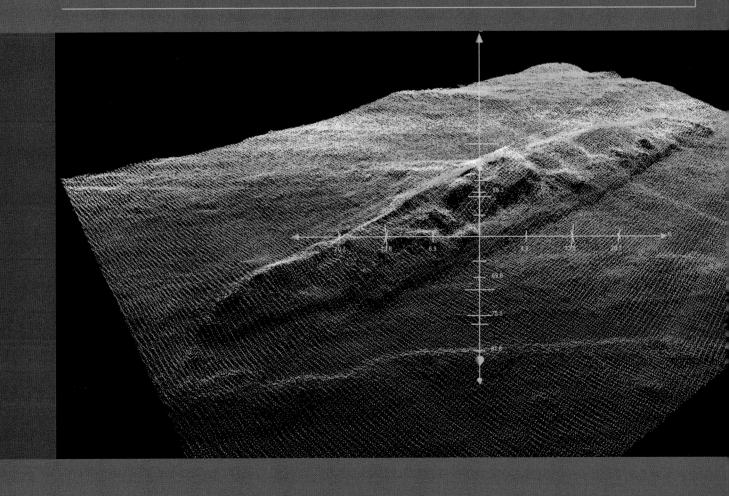

Diving & Investigation

Salvage, Diving and Investigation of the Wreck Site Through Time

Perhaps the allure of the wreck of the RMS *Lusitania* to divers, salvors and other diving interests is best explained in diver Gary Gentile's two volume book *The Lusitania Controversies*, where he states:

> "The *Lusitania* is one of the most notorious shipwrecks in seafaring history, not only because of the circumstances of her sinking – the result of a German torpedo – or because of the enormous loss of life that resulted, but because the wreck has come to symbolize what is achievable in the realm of underwater exploration."
>
> (1999, Vol. 2, dust jacket)

The wreck became the focus of attention for divers in the decade immediately after it was lost, for a variety of reasons. Some sought to salvage its cargo, including munitions and arms, but they were also inspired by tales of gold, silver, rare paintings or valuables locked in the purser's safe. Others sought to identify if it was carrying illicit armaments while also looking to answer the enduring question of what caused the second explosion. In more recent times, with the advent of technical sports diving, the site has become a key component on many recreational divers' wish lists of deepwater and iconic wrecks in the world that have to be dived. To those who dive the site it can mean many things but what is clear is that the history of diving on the wreck site has now become a significant part of the history of the wreck itself.

In 1982, Ireland's territorial waters were extended to the 12-mile limit. Previously, the wreck of the *Lusitania* lay in international waters and thus outside the jurisdiction of the Irish State. With the extension of

Gregg Bemis, owner of the *Lusitania*, chats to divers in 2002 prior to them descending to the wreck 93m below the surface. (Photo Karl Brady)

the territorial waters, the wreck falls under the governance of both the Merchant Shipping (Salvage and Wreck) Act 1894, as amended in 1993, and the National Monuments (Amendment) Acts of 1987 and 1994. The latter Act specifically protects shipwrecks over 100 years old but also allows for the protection of wrecks less than that age which have a particular historical significance. This facilitated the placing of an Underwater Heritage Order on the wreck in 1995 by the then Minister for Arts, Culture and the Gaeltacht Michael D. Higgins, to ensure its protection and preservation. Being over 100 years old now, all provisions of the 1987 Act apply to the wreck.

Using technical diving equipment, recreational divers prepare to dive the wreck. (Photo Karl Brady)

Ten .303 bullets recovered from one of the liner's forward cargo holds by divers in 2008. (Photo Connie Kelleher)

Early salvage efforts

In 1922 the German Nationalist Party put a parliamentary question to the Reichstag seeking clarification on an Anglo-American company that had been recently formed to carry out salvage, including the removal of "ammunition, torpedoes and two submarines" from the wreck of the *Lusitania* (*The Manchester Guardian* 1st July 1922, 15). If such cargo could be verified it could serve to legitimise the German targeting of the vessel in 1915. The Party was concerned that the cargo was to be removed as a way of bolstering continuing anti-German sentiment and sought to have a German expert present when the salvage operation was being undertaken (*ibid.*). This followed an article published in the *Observer* newspaper titled "Can the *Lusitania* be raised?". It reported that America hoped to raise the wreck, and a salvage company registered as the *Lusitania* Salvage Company of Philadelphia, was at that stage travelling to the Irish coast to begin operations. Sir Frederick Young, then in charge of the UK Admiralty Salvage Section, viewed the proposed project with particular scepticism, stating that:

> "It will be gathered, therefore, that the *Lusitania* Salvage Company of Philadelphia has a very difficult, if not an impossible, task before it, and that in any case the enterprise will require the support of philanthropists or of persons who would not mind what money they lose in the hope

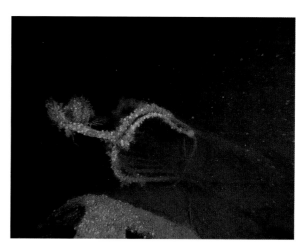

Photo taken from above of a bathtub and integrated shower which originally would have formed part of the comforts of a first-class cabin. (Photo Barry McGill)

Diver inspects a window from a first-class cabin. (Photo Barry McGill)

of ascertaining all that happened to the torpedoed liner."

(*The Observer* 14th May 1922, 9)

Sir Frederick Young's comments, particularly to do with the level of financial backing needed for such an operation and, indeed, in relation to the mystery over what sank the liner, were indeed prophetic and relevant to the present day plans for the exploration of the wreck.

Naval and other official activity

Some diving may have been undertaken on the wreck by the Royal Navy soon after the ship sank, but this was never fully verified. Immediately following the sinking of the *Lusitania*, the shallowest part of the wreck would have been about 65m below the surface and thus relatively accessible for diving on air. In 1920 a Liverpool salvage company visited the wreck site and may have been acting on behalf of the insurers, Liverpool and War Risks. The company only had the use of a small steamer, however, and even though it spent two summers at the site, little is known of its work and it is believed little was achieved (Bourke 1998, 190–191).

During the 1940s and 1950s unsubstantiated reports came out that the Royal Navy, under orders of the British Admiralty, depth charged the wreck site on a number of occasions. Reports suggested that the Royal Navy vessel *Reclaim* was used for these operations to destroy unexploded ordnance and to test the effectiveness of submarine bombs. Another report posited that it was targeting a Russian submarine hiding in the shadow of the wreck of the *Lusitania* and yet another that it was with a view to concealing the quantity of munitions that could be seen on the wreck site. While the identification of hedgehog bombs on the wreck site by Oceaneering in 1982 (see below) could provide evidence for this or indeed later activity by the Irish Navy, specific details are not available as to what actually took place on the site during this period (*ibid.*, 192–193).

Diver in a one-atmosphere diving suit or Newtsuit being deployed from the deck of the ILV *Granuaile* during the 2011 National Geographic expedition. (Photo Karl Brady)

Salvage ship Ophir and 'Tritonia' Diving Armour

While it was indicated in plans for raising the wreck in 1922 that its general location was known, it was not until 1935, when the salvage ship *Ophir* carried out grapple sweep surveys in the area, that the wreck site was positively relocated. Diver Jim Jarrett successfully reached the wreck in that year on behalf of the salvage company, using a one-atmosphere diving suit. This newly developed 'apparatus suitable for treasure salvaging' and named the 'Tritonia' Diving Armour, was invented by Joseph Salim Peress. Jarrett, being Peress' chief diver, only carried out one dive on the site, however, with the dive being more a trial of the suit than an investigation of the wreck itself (Ballard 1995, 209). Also in 1935, a report in *The Times* newspaper refers to activity by Italian salvage company Sorima in Irish waters and the discovery of two wrecks by the salvage vessels, *Artiglio* and *Rampino*, while undertaking drag surveying in the general area. The first wreck was found at a depth of 300ft, "near where the *Lusitania* sank" and the second wreck "may be the *Lincolnshire* which is the wreck that the company was searching for. At the same time, another of the Company's salvage ships, the *Arpione*, was involved in the recovery of brass and copper from the wreck of the steamship *Ludgate*, wrecked off Galley Head in Cork in the year 1917" (*The Times* 28th September 1935, 14).

Underwater cameraman John Light

It was not until the 1960s that more targeted investigation relating to the cause of the ship's sinking took place. Described as a 'swashbuckling ex-US Navy diver', John Light retired from the US Navy and went on to build a career for himself as an underwater cameraman. He worked for NBC Television News which was interested in filming the wreck of the *Lusitania*. Thus Light's interest in diving married well with his work and he pursued his interest in investigating the nature of the munitions that were on board the ill-fated liner, in the hope of filming the evidence if he could find it. While he spent two years diving the site with a team of divers on compressed air and pushed the safety limits for diving at such depths to the extremes he did not find the evidence that he was seeking. John Light, in 1967, finally purchased the wreck of the *Lusitania* from the War Risks Association of Liverpool, for a sum of £1,000, but this was for the hull, machinery and appurtenances only. It did not include any cargo or the personal possessions of the passengers or crew (O'Sullivan 2014, 4–5). He then began a much more ambitious project, kitting out a dedicated salvage vessel and seeking to undertake a substantial recovery project on the wreck site. A number of financial backers came on board to share the costs of the operation, including initially a Boston building contractor named George Macomber who was later joined by American businessman and now owner of the wreck, F. Gregg Bemis. John Light's grand plan never materialised, running into insurmountable financial difficulties and time delays. He died in 1992 but not before he had carried out crucial historical research into contemporary accounts of the sinking, research that has influenced many subsequent publications on the wreck of the Cunard liner (*ibid.*, 11–12).

Oceaneering

Oceaneering International Inc., a subsea engineering and technology company based in Houston, Texas,

The telemotor from the *Lusitania* recovered by Eoin McGarry in 2011 following the National Geographic expedition. (Courtesy of Laurence Dunne Archaeology)

carried out the largest salvage operation on the wreck of the *Lusitania* in 1982 (Gentile 1999, 216–223). Oceaneering raised a significant amount of artefacts, including smaller items such as the signal bell, one of the steam whistles, various portholes, brass windows, a carved wooden balustrade, Wedgwood plates, glassware, marble pillar bases, buttons, silver and gold watches, forks, knives and spoons. Larger objects included three of the four huge bronze propellers and two 20-ton anchors from the ship (*ibid.*, 219–220). One of the propellers now sits outside the Merseyside Maritime Museum in Liverpool while another was melted down and reforged into 3,500 golf clubs that were then sold to the highest bidders. Of the various types of munitions recovered, none indicated that the *Lusitania* was carrying any arms beyond what was listed on its manifest. While some items were donated to the Merseyside Museum, most were sold off but the monies raised were not sufficient to defray the overall cost of the salvage operations.

The question of title to objects recovered from the wreck in 1982 and brought into the United Kingdom was considered by the English Courts in the case of *Pierce v Bemis (The Lusitania)* [1986] 1 Q.B. 384 (see also Reeder 2003, 289–290). It was held that, in the absence of the true owners, the persons who had recovered objects which had been personal property of the passengers or part of the cargo had good title to them. It should be noted that the case dealt with a set of objects actually recovered and the decision depended on the fact that the United Kingdom

Bell recovered from the wreck during the 1982 expedition and now housed in the Maritime Museum, Greenwich. (Courtesy of the Imperial War Museum)

A submersible being deployed from the ILV *Granuaile* during the 2011 National Geographic expedition to the *Lusitania*. (Photo Fionnbarr Moore)

legislation as it then stood (section 523 of the Merchant Shipping Act 1894) was interpreted as limiting Crown title to unclaimed wrecks found in United Kingdom territorial waters.

Robert Ballard and National Geographic Society

In 1993 perhaps the first truly scientific investigation of the *Lusitania* was carried out. Scientist and Commander Robert Ballard of Woods Hole Oceanographic Institute in association with National Geographic and with approval from the owner, F. Gregg Bemis, carried out unmanned diving surveys of the wreck. Using various forms of cutting-edge technology, including ROVs (remotely operated vehicles) and submersibles, they were able to map the wreck in its entirety. An impressive documentary resulted from the two weeks on site and both video and photographic results are still among the best images taken of the wreck site. From the investigations carried out, including a survey of the entire area where the magazine was located, Ballard was able to show that the area had remained undamaged. He concluded that if it had contained illicit munitions, they were not the cause of a second explosion. A boiler explosion was also dismissed based on the earlier testimony of three of the surviving boiler stokers, who reported never hearing an explosion from that area. Ballard put forward a new theory based on evidence from scattered coal on the seabed – that when the torpedo struck, it did so below the waterline in the area where the coal bunkers were located and thus ignited the coal dust there (Ballard 1995, 194).

Technical sports divers

During the period after Ballard carried out his expedition, the wreck became a popular dive site for recreational divers using newly developed diving technology. Mixed-gas diving has allowed sports divers to dive deeper than ever before. This method was pioneered by veteran wreck diver Gary Gentile who was also one of the key members of Starfish Enterprise, the dive group formed by fellow diver Polly Tapson in 1993 to dive the *Lusitania*. Their dive did not take place until 1994, when Tapson and her international team spent a week on the wreck site. Gentile (1999, 224–301) gives a vivid account of their time on the wreck in his book and includes an equally detailed account of their legal argument with the owner of the wreck F. Gregg Bemis, who had not given the divers permission to dive the site. Mr Bemis' concerns for the safety of the wreck and the diving taking place at the time, including his representations to the Irish Government, led in no small way to the placing of the Underwater Heritage Order on the site in 1995 to ensure its protection under the National Monuments (Amendment) Act of 1987.

Des Quigley of Irish Technical Divers also dived the *Lusitania* in 1994 and on several occasions thereafter, on behalf of the wreck's owner. Mr Quigley was the first to carry out a rebreather dive on the site (Bourke 1998, 194). From 2000 to the present day, an average of one to two dive excursions by technical sports divers are undertaken on the wreck site each year. These are licensed by the State and, when the need arises, are monitored by archaeologists from the National Monuments Service. In the early 2000s,

2006 expedition to the wreck by Cork-based diver Pat Glavin and his team, who were the first to come across the .303 bullets which were recovered in 2008. (Photo Connie Kelleher)

several UK-based divers dived the wreck but consistently dive teams have become more Irish based, with some teams including those led by Cork-based diver Pat Glavin, Mayo-based diver Pat Coughlan and Waterford native Eoin McGarry being those most frequently leading dives to the site in recent years.

2008 Discovery Channel and Odyssey Marine Exploration

In July 2008, the deep-ocean maritime salvage company Odyssey Marine Exploration carried out non-invasive survey at the wreck site. In conjunction with the wreck's owner, F. Gregg Bemis, and funded by the Discovery Channel whose film crew was on board the company's ship *Odyssey Explorer*, the week-long work involved detailed surveys comprising bathymetry, ROV and photographic survey, the purpose of which was to seek answers to the cause of the second explosion. Carried out under licence from the State, the project was inspected by members of the Irish Navy and the National Monuments Service. While high-quality geophysical data and photographic imagery were obtained, no evidence was found to support the theory that the ship was secretly carrying excessive amounts of munitions above that listed on its manifest.

2011 National Geographic returns

In 2011 F. Gregg Bemis, in association with National Geographic Channel, Bowler Bill Entertainment

(Bowler Bill being a nick name for Captain Turner) and technical diver Eoin McGarry, carried out an extensive dive expedition over a period of 10 days. For the first time ever the project team included two archaeologists; maritime archaeologist Laurence Dunne and underwater archaeologist Julianna O'Donoghue were key to devising the scientific methodology, which in turn informed the diving and investigation of the wreck site. This covered the proposed cutting of a section of the steel hull to gain access to the wreck and enable investigation of an area that might provide evidence for the second explosion or the nature of munitions on board. The archaeological brief also involved monitoring the recovery of a number of agreed artefacts from the wreck itself. National Geographic engaged the services of Nuytco Research Ltd of Vancouver, Canada, and they also had the use of their two-person Dual Deep Worker submersible as well as their one-atmosphere Newtsuit. Using the Irish Lights vessel *Granuaile*, the dive team successfully deployed their diver in the Newtsuit but he was unable to remove part of the steel hull due to the strength of the rivets still holding the steel plate in place. A number of artefacts were successfully recovered, however, including one of the telemotors, a telltale and a number of portholes. As part of the archaeological oversight, an agreed conservation strategy was in place for the artefacts and conservator Ian Panter of York Archaeological Trust undertook the conservation of the material thereafter (Dunne 2013).

Over the years, and particularly in recent times with the improvement in dive equipment that allows deeper dives to be carried out, the *Lusitania* has seen divers return to the site on several occasions. The lure of the wreck is one that is communally felt among sports divers but each dive on the site is also a very personal one for each diver. Perhaps this enticement and excitement is best understood when reading some personal accounts by individual divers who have chosen to revisit the site and have re-engaged over time with the remains of the *Lusitania*.

Personal Insights: Diving the Lusitania

Stewart Andrews (Technical Diver and Dalkey SAC): Permanent etchings in one's memory

Diving the '*Lusi*', as it is regularly referred to by divers, is often seen as one of the pinnacles in a diver's career. In this part of the world, it is the second best known wreck site, after RMS *Titanic,* and has the advantage of being diveable – albeit the preserve of so-called 'technical divers'. At a depth of 93m, the *Lusitania* presents formidable challenges. Very few divers use standard open-circuit scuba cylinders for dives deeper than 70m these days, due to the high cost of helium (to reduce the drunken effect of nitrogen narcosis) and the severe limitation on time underwater. For the past decade or so, divers chose to dive these depths using mixed-gas rebreather technology, where the gas breathed is continuously recycled – with the gas being scrubbed or cleaned of the exhaled carbon dioxide and the depleted oxygen replenished. It takes years of gradually pushing your training and experience to get to these depths – this in itself is another challenge and deep sports divers pay the price in terms of costly equipment, training and going on work-up expeditions. Dive times of 50 minutes at 90+m are not unknown today – and decompressing (eliminating inert gases absorbed at that depth) means a slowed ascent back to the surface, lasting over five hours!

And then there is the underwater visibility, or 'vis' in diver-speak, which at this location typically varies between 2m and 8m – the latter on an exceptionally good day. With a distinct level of apprehension amongst the divers, the skipper drops you upstream of a buoyed shot-line to the wreck. As you float down the line (or pull your way down in a current!), you visualise the dive to come. It takes about five minutes to travel down to the bottom. With the excitement and anticipation of the dive rising, you must allow plenty of time during your descent to check gas pressures and keep your eye on the workings of the rebreather as it tries to keep you alive by giving you a viable breathing mixture for your current depth. Once on the bottom, you start to orientate yourself, with the knowledge that the wreck lies to starboard (on her right hand side, looking forward). With visibility in the region of 2–3m, most divers will elect to run a piece of line from a reel, starting at the shot and belaying it around steelwork to keep it taut. It is important to return to the shot-line as this gets you back to the other divers and possible open-circuit gas in the rare event that your rebreather fails – there is safety in numbers. It also allows for a more pleasant decompression on the ascent on the horizontal bars of the pre-deployed deco-station.

Quickly your eyes adjust to the low light levels and the various shapes – an impressive oblong brass porthole with a filigree vent on top, a circular porthole, steam whistles, bollards with the original mooring warps wrapped around them, a winch, that massive anchor chain and finally the bow and that prominent stem. On the return journey, you detour a bit to find the captain's first-class bath with its copper and brass framework for the shower nozzles – and yes, the workmanship was so good that the rose shower-head is still in place; what a rare and beautiful sight for any diver. On subsequent dives, you ask the skipper to drop the shot in other places close to the site of this massive, 240m-long wreck with a view to coming down perhaps at mid-ships where the wreck lies in a state of partial collapse at one of the dining areas, and pewter serving dishes with their covers intact can be seen; you can't believe your luck to see such items, last used on this ocean liner over 100 years ago.

Another dive at the stern allows you to travel past the mooring bollards and fairleads, then over the high port side of the stern to the hull plates on the outer part of the ship. Dropping down towards the seabed where the stub of the propeller shaft, which was crudely but quite cleanly 'cut' using explosives during the 1982 salvage works, is visible. When recovered, the massive bronze propeller was melted down and reforged to make golf clubs, of all things! Travelling down the 'tunnel' that forms the hull shapes between the propeller shafts, you can just see two bronze blade tips of the remaining propeller – obviously considered too difficult to salvage due to the weight of the ship's stern lying on it. A low point of the dive is turning around in this dead-end to find that the 'vis' has gone from 3m to almost zero due to one's own finning action… it is enough to focus the mind as you extend an arm to follow the hull steelwork back up and out to clearer water and emerging brightness.

A thrilling end to a thrilling series of dives – not just one for the logbook, but also for those permanent etchings in one's memory.

Personal Insights: Diving the Lusitania

Pat Coughlan (Technical Diver & Granuaile SAC): Diving the Lusitania

When diving the *Lusitania* a diver faces not only the physical challenges of the dive but also the logistical challenges; divers worldwide regard the *Lusitania* as an iconic wreck not least because of the history and controversy surrounding her sinking but also because of the depth and bottom conditions. In a little more than 90m of water the *Lusitania* is well beyond the scope of recreational scuba divers and was for many years the preserve of only commercial and military divers. In the 1970s a team of divers conducted a series of scuba dives but had very limited bottom time and the divers suffered from the narcotic effect of using air at depth. To enable divers to push depth limits and bottom times, technical diving evolved. This may best be described as using equipment, techniques and gases (helium) to enable the diver to push beyond 40m depth and extend bottom times, but in so doing it exposes them to significantly increased risks.

In 1994 two diving teams – one Irish, one international – were the first to conduct a series of technical dives on the *Lusitania* using 'trimix' gas (a blend of oxygen, nitrogen and helium) using scuba equipment. The introduction of helium reduced the narcotic effect of nitrogen at depth. The time spent on the bottom, however, was limited by the capacity of their cylinders. In the 1990s these dives were regarded as extreme, but now standards in deep diving, equipment, techniques and training have evolved to the degree that 100m dives are regularly conducted, though still not without risk. The most significant development in technical diving in recent years has been the introduction of commercially available closed circuit rebreathers that have enabled divers to significantly increase their time on the bottom. As an example, divers regularly conduct 30-minute dives on the bottom at the wreck site; however, this does require over 2 hours 30 minutes decompression on the way back up before the surface is reached. Rebreathers work by reusing the diver's exhaled breath, instead of venting to the surface in the form of bubbles. The expelled air enters a carbon dioxide scrubber where the carbon dioxide is removed out of the breathing gas, oxygen sensors measure the oxygen content and electronics monitor the addition of oxygen to maintain the optimum oxygen level for the depth.

Successfully diving to the depth of the *Lusitania* over a period of days also presents logistical challenges that have to be addressed prior to diving to ensure both smooth operations and safe diving. As part of the pre-dive planning, in the first instance, an experienced dive team needs to be assembled. A Dive Licence application has to be submitted to the National Monuments Service, under the terms of the National Monuments Act and the permission of the owner of the wreck, Mr F. Gregg Bemis, is required. As part of the Dive Licence application process, an overview of the proposed dive is attached to the application, which can include, but is not limited to risk assessment, method plan, tides, dive vessel, weather, bottom conditions and equipment. While there are challenges, serious safety considerations and multiple logistical elements involved – seeing the remains of this once great liner up close is always rewarding when carrying out any expedition to 'dive the *Lucy*'.

Mapping the Seabed & Shipwrecks in Irish Waters

Validating Visualisation

The value of and interest in the mapping of shipwrecks in Irish waters, particularly those from the era of the two World Wars, has been highlighted in the publication *Warships, U-Boats and Liners* (Brady *et al.* 2012), with the popularity of the publication endorsing the audience appeal of mapping, imaging and informing on these long lost vessels. Similarly, INFOMAR's wreck data sheets, downloadable from the main website, have proven hugely popular, particularly with the diving fraternity. They not only provide individual wreck information and mapping imagery that is easily accessible and understandable, placing each wreck within its geographical location, but they also serve to place these lost ships within the context of the maritime landscape around the Irish coast. Zones of wrecking are highlighted, and an overview of the wreck data for the area as well as the mapping and cultural information on the individual shipwrecks is given for each zone. In this way the INFOMAR wreck mapping data dovetails perfectly with the information contained in the Wreck Inventory of Ireland Database held by the National Monuments Service and continues this close collaboration between the two departments.

Elsewhere, the mapping of shipwrecks is similarly being done, with striking results – not least that of some of the WWI German High Seas fleet, scuttled at Scapa Flow in June 1919 (Dean & Rowland 2007). These highlight the advances that have been made in deep-sea mapping technology providing advanced results in visualisation and imagery. INFOMAR, too, has advanced its mapping capabilities, with recent surveys undertaken by the Marine Institute, in collaboration with colleagues in the University of Ulster and the Department of the Environment, Northern Ireland, on some wrecks along the east coast of Ireland. The results of their surveys can be viewed as 3D interactive models on the website (https://www.infomar.ie/maps/downloadable-maps/shipwrecks). From its inception as the Irish National Seabed Survey in 1999, and subsequent evolution to the INtegrated Mapping FOr the Sustainable Development of Ireland's MArine Resource in 2006, INFOMAR has continually advanced its techniques and capabilities in the field of seabed mapping, including the identification and visualisation of shipwrecks.

INFOMAR's Mapping Programme

The INFOMAR programme, funded by the Department of Communications, Climate Action and Environment, completed phase 1 in the first half of 2016. INFOMAR's initial focus was on 26 bays and three priority areas for its first 10 years of operation (phase 1), with these areas being identified during an extensive stakeholder exercise that was conducted between 2002 and 2005. This exercise included consultation with over 50 organisations, government departments, coastal local authorities, industry sectors and consultancy companies. During that period the EU-designated Biologically Sensitive Area was also surveyed on an opportunistic basis, e.g. where use of vessels such as the RV *Celtic Explorer* could be used to best effect by taking part of this area while also working on a priority area. Phase II of INFOMAR's

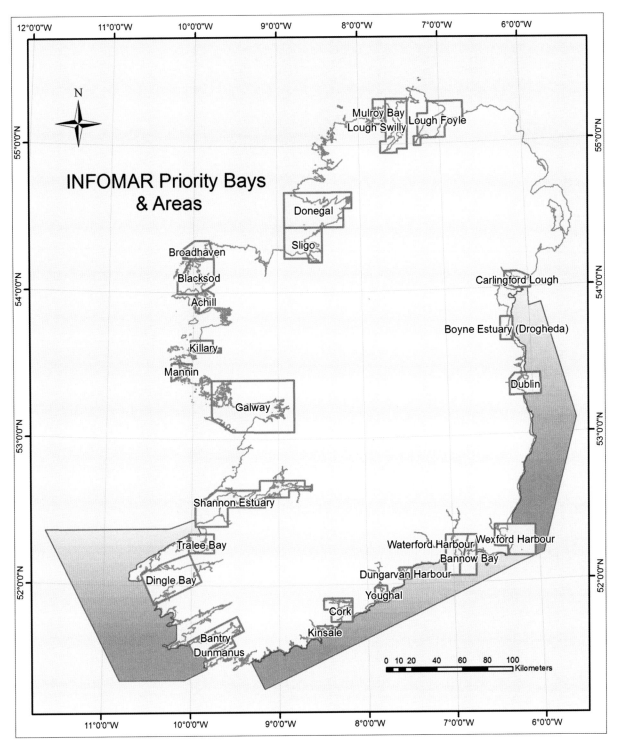

INFOMAR Phase 1 (2006–2016) priority bays and areas.

The RV *Keary* – the Geological Survey Ireland inshore research vessel for INFOMAR near-shore survey.

mapping programme commenced in mid-2016 and is intended to run for a further 10 years. Mapping to approximately the 200m contour, by the end of 2005 the Irish National Seabed Survey achieved a total mapping coverage of 432,000km² of the seas around Ireland. By that year over 81% of the Irish designated seabed area was mapped and the Irish National Seabed Survey's work delivered a national asset that has provided Ireland with a dataset to underpin present and future economic, environmental, infrastructural, social and policy issues. This has been underscored by significant capacity building, both in terms of Irish marine surveying infrastructure and the development of personnel skilled in the design, planning, implementation and management of a large-scale integrated marine resource evaluation programme. Following the completion of the Irish National Seabed Survey programme of works, INFOMAR began surveying the waters that remain to be mapped around the coast of Ireland. But more than that, INFOMAR is also delivering an enhanced data management and delivery service for data gathered

under both the Irish National Seabed Survey and INFOMAR. This data delivery strategy is intended to promote the creation of value added products.

Survey Vessels

A wide range of vessels is used during the INFOMAR programme to undertake geophysical surveys. Water depth is a determining factor for which type of vessel should be used. The Marine Institute vessels, RV *Celtic Explorer* and RV *Celtic Voyager*, map the deeper bays and areas while the Geological Survey Ireland vessel the RV *Keary* (named after Raymond Keary, one of Ireland's pioneering marine geologists) maps shallower areas, those under 20m. This vessel has completed most of the shallow water surveys since commencing work in these areas in 2009. The MV *Cosantóir Bradán*, an Inland Fisheries Ireland vessel, was re-launched as a marine survey vessel in 2012 and along with the RV *Geo*, a 7.5m rib, has formed part of the INFOMAR mapping programme since. In 2015 the Geological Survey Ireland launched a new 7.9m Cheetah

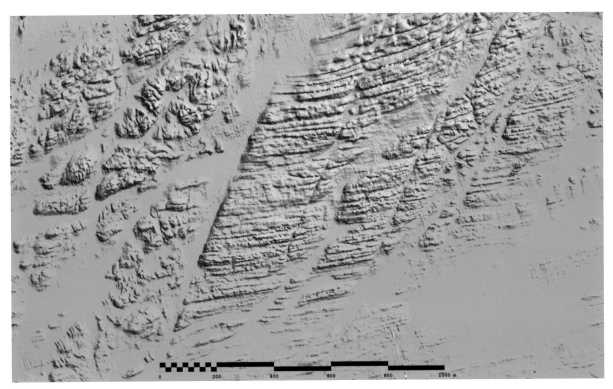

A plan view of rocky seabed containing the site of a shipwreck. Shipwrecks are often hard to visualise on the vast ocean floor especially if uncharted or located in such terrain. However, detailed processing and examination of the data can help reveal the location and extent of low profile wreck remains on the seabed. See the following two images for further detail on processing multibeam data.

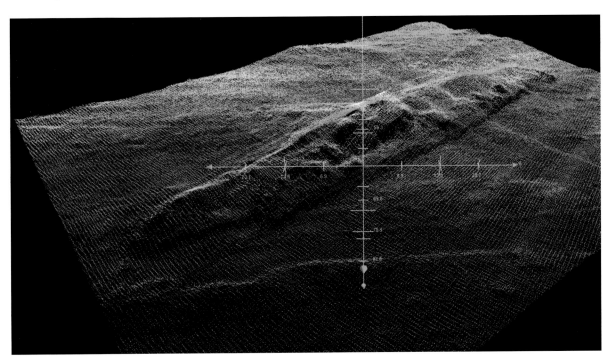

Multibeam data needs to be processed and refined in order to fully visualise a wreck in high resolution. This image shows the wreck in a point cloud format (each point representing a depth sounding) prior to being gridded and fully processed (see overleaf for image of fully processed/gridded image).

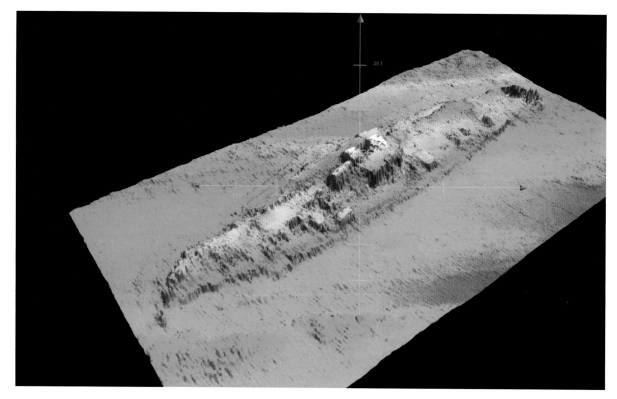

A 3D view of the 'gridded' multibeam data to show the shipwreck at a resolution of up to 10cm (one depth sounding every 10cm). The image shows SS *Miami* which was lost in 1917 southeast of Baltimore, County Cork. The wreck was surveyed by the RV *Celtic Voyager* in 2014.

catamaran to complete the remaining shallow water areas within 5 of the 26 priority bays. These vessels facilitate multibeam and shallow seismic surveys as well as ground truthing, side scan sonar and ROV operations.

Data Acquisition Systems

To date over 400 surveyed shipwrecks have been recorded in the INFOMAR shipwreck inventory which originated from the work carried out under the Irish National Seabed Survey. The database comprises accurately located shipwrecks (known, unknown and in some cases uncharted), containing detailed information regarding each wreck's condition on the seafloor, its extent, dimensions and water depth. This is made possible by means of high-resolution multibeam data acquired over the site of the wreck. The multibeam data is processed using a variety of hydrographic software, and 2D and 3D imaging is achievable, in some cases to a resolution of 10cm. Over the past 13

years the multibeam systems used to map Irish waters have varied from deepwater systems to those designed for shallow water surveys. In moving from deep to shallow waters the systems used have advanced to produce higher resolution mapping. These advancements have in turn aided the development of imaging shipwrecks in greater detail.

A variety of multibeam echosounder (MBES) systems are used in order to acquire bathymetric data. The type of system used has moved from deepwater systems such as the Kongsberg Simrad EM120 and EM1002 to systems designed for shallow water surveys such as the Kongsberg EM3002, EM2040, Reson 7101 and more recently a Reson T20P, R2sonic T24. At a basic level, the hull-mounted MBES transducers emit sound at a given frequency that travels down through the water column. As it is a high frequency sound wave, when it reaches the seabed most is reflected back towards the surface where sensors record the returning sound wave. An MBES's main function is to use acoustic energy to calculate depth. However, MBESs such as the Kongsberg EM2040 also collect additional information, including the strength of the acoustic signal (or return) from the seafloor. This is known as backscatter. Differing seafloor types, such as mud, sand, gravel and rock will have different backscatter values depending on the amount of energy they return to the sonar head. Rocky areas will typically have high returns while soft sediments like mud are more likely to absorb energy and have low backscatter returns. These differing values are used to generate a grey-order image (i.e. dark for high returns, bright for low returns) of the seabed which can be used to examine the nature of the seafloor or wrecks that lie on the seafloor.

Single Beam Echosounders (SBES) work on a similar principle to the MBES. In the case of the SBES, however, acoustic energy is directed straight down from the hull of the vessel as opposed to the swath of beams seen in MBES. This means that water depth measurements can only be made along the ship's track with a single beam. As a result, the output data from an SBES is in profile form compared to the area

coverage from an MBES and details for shipwreck mapping purposes may be limited. Operating at lower frequencies than the MBES, the energy from a Shallow Seismic Pinger/Sub Bottom Profiler is both reflected from and penetrates through the seabed. The sound that penetrates through the seafloor may be reflected due to density changes within the sediments. The result is a series of sound waves returning to the survey vessel at slightly different times depending on how deep they penetrated through the sediment before returning. These are displayed in the pinger output as a series of layers that can be interpreted to reveal past sedimentation patterns for the area or importantly, buried cultural material, including paleo-landscapes, shipwrecks, etc. Data quality of the pinger is dependent on sediment type (good through sands, poor through gravels and bedrock) and gas content (poor through gaseous sediments).

In contrast to the pinger system a side scan sonar uses sound waves directed perpendicular to the direction of travel to 'see' the seafloor on either side of

RV *Celtic Voyager* returning to harbour after completing another successful survey.

the towed fish. The result is an image where the central area beneath the fish is blanked out by the returning sound. Moving away from this centre line, objects and features on the seabed are picked up to produce relatively detailed images of the seafloor. The combined use of some or all of the data acquisition systems by INFOMAR during its mapping project has ensured the discovery of new wrecks, mapping of previously known wrecks, and critically, has provided detail on many wrecks not previously seen.

Imaging Shipwrecks

Having acquired MBES data the process of getting the raw data to a map begins. INFOMAR predominately uses specialised hydrographic processing software called Caris Hips & Sips to do this. The raw MBES data is corrected for positioning, navigational, sound velocity and tidal factors which produce bathymetric data levelled to the Lowest Astronomical Tide datum. Once these corrections have been applied the data is 'cleaned' to remove such factors as noise, spikes and artefacts (false soundings or depth readings due to interference to the multibeam equipment from other systems on board) which are logged during real time data acquisition. The processed data is then exported into various XYZ formats to create products such as shaded relief charts and bathymetric surfaces.

The imaging of shipwrecks is something that can be either straightforward, if the position of the wreck is previously known, or at times a challenging task. To an untrained eye the position of an unknown or uncharted shipwreck may resemble that of an anomaly or rock outcrop lying on the seabed. Often on closer inspection this 'anomaly' can actually be a wreck. The high-resolution MBES data allows for 2D and 3D softwares to 'grid' the soundings data to surfaces at resolutions often as high as 10cm. To meet hydrographic standards a minimum of four survey lines must be acquired over a wreck site. This in turn usually provides sufficient data density to produce high-quality MBES images of shipwrecks on the seabed.

Mapping WWI Wrecks

World War I was a bloody and brutal conflict which resulted in the loss of up to 17 million lives and had long-lasting economic, social and political consequences which continue to reverberate to this day. The conflict was not confined to the main theatres of war in Continental Europe, Africa and the Middle East, but also saw a vicious campaign of naval conflict on the high seas resulting in the loss of thousands of lives and ships on both sides. While many of these wrecks lie dotted around the globe, the waters around Ireland and Britain did not escape this conflict as both Britain and Germany attempted to starve each other into submission through naval blockades and a deadly submarine offensive by Germany. It is estimated that up to 1,000 wrecks dating to this period lie within Ireland's Designated Waters, with up to 400 of these vessels lost close to shore and within the 12-mile territorial limit. Apart from being a tangible and visceral reminder of the terrible events which took place 100 years ago, the high numbers of lives lost graphically illustrate that, apart from being significant underwater heritage sites in their own right, many of these wrecks are essentially war graves deserving of our respect and treated accordingly.

As well as forming an important element of Irish maritime heritage, WWI shipwrecks are also inextricably linked to the heritage of the many different countries which were involved, both directly and indirectly, in the global conflict, a fact reflected in the high number of foreign vessels sunk in Irish waters. It is through locating, mapping, studying and preserving such wrecks that the reality of the events of the time can be more fully understood and appreciated, not least the tragedy and loss that unfolded in the coastal waters of Ireland when the North Atlantic and Irish Sea were theatres of war. While an overview of this conflict is presented in Section 3 (pp 37–45), the following pages provide some insights into a small number of wrecks lost during this period that have been mapped by INFOMAR in recent years.

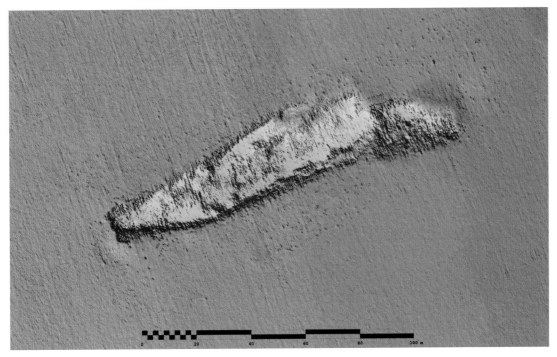

SS Feltria

Located 22km south of Tramore, the 5,254-ton SS *Feltria* lies in two pieces and is orientated in a NE/SW direction on the seabed. The wreck measures 130m x 25m and lies at a depth of 63m. It was built in 1891 by W. Denny and Bros and was owned by Cunard SS Company. The 26-year-old ship was torpedoed without warning on 5th May 1917 by German submarine *UC-48* while en route from New York to Avonmouth and suffered a loss of 45 crew. The postcard above (Lawler Collection) shows the *Feltria* docked in London when it was called the SS *Uranium* (1910–1916) and owned by the Uranium Steamship Company.

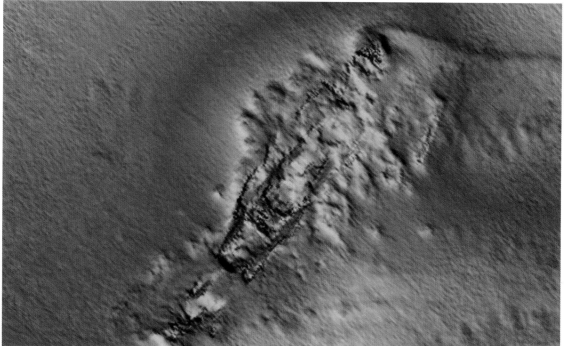

SS Seang Choon

Lying 1.3km south of Mizen Head off County Cork, the wreck of the 5,807-ton steamship SS *Seang Choon* lies at a general depth of 87m. It measures 140m x 28m on the seabed and is relatively intact, though largely buried. Debris is scattered around the wreck itself and several scours surround the main structure. The passenger liner was built by Harland and Wolff in 1891 as the *Cheshire* for Bibby Lines and was originally owned by Lim Chin Tsong of Rangoon but requisitioned by the British Government a few months before it was sunk. It was torpedoed by the *U-87* while en route from Sydney to London with a general cargo of 400 tons of copper and 601 tons of lead; 19 lives were lost. Risdon Beazley salvaged most of the copper and lead in 1958. (Ian Lawler Collection)

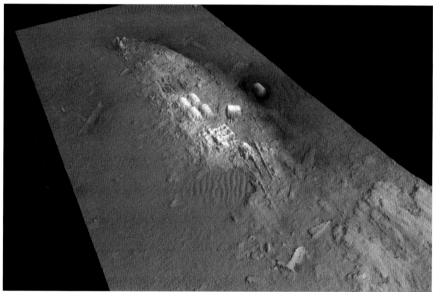

SS Laurentic

The *Laurentic* was a 14,892-ton liner built in 1908 by Harland and Wolff and owned by the Oceanic Steam Navigation Company. At the beginning of the war, the liner was hired by the White Star Line and converted into an armed merchant cruiser. The steamship was en route from Liverpool to Halifax via Buncrana in County Donegal, from where it departed on 25th January 1917, but struck a mine and sank with the loss of 354 lives. Many of the bodies were recovered and were buried in St Mura's graveyard in Fahan where a memorial was erected to them in 1919. The ship was carrying a cargo of gold for the British Treasury, which was to be used to purchase arms, munitions and vital supplies for the war effort. A total of 3,186 of the 3,211 gold bars on board were recovered during subsequent salvage operations following its sinking. What remains of the wreck measures 140m in length by 25m in breath and lies at an average height off the seabed of c. 5m. The RV *Keary* surveyed the wreck in 2014. The postcard above shows a painting of the *Laurentic* under steam prior to the beginning of the war (Ian Lawler Collection). The wreck now lies at an average depth of c. 37m in a slight scour and is partially buried, with collapsed structure and a significant debris field surrounding it. The multibeam image clearly shows four of the six boilers are still *in-situ*; however, two have been dislodged and have been rolled out to the starboard side of the wreck by the Atlantic swells.

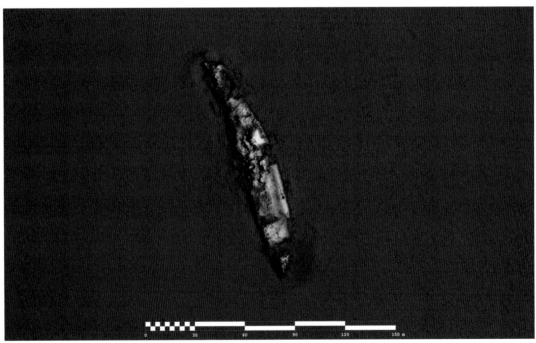

Antony

A 6,446-ton, twin-screw steam liner owned by Booth Line of Liverpool, was employed on the passenger and mail service between Britain, Argentina and Brazil. At the time of its loss, the *Antony* was travelling from Belém in Brazil to Liverpool, with four passengers, 126 crewmen and a cargo of rubber. It was unaware that the *UC-48* was patrolling the southwest coast of Ireland, when, without warning, the submarine torpedoed the liner on the 17th March 1917, striking its port side. Fifty-five lives were lost. The wreck lies at a general depth of 53m and is located c. 15m southeast of Dunmore East. It measures 133m x 22m and is largely intact. The RV *Celtic Voyager* surveyed the site in 2013. The black and white photo above shows the *Antony* under steam during one of its transatlantic voyages. (Ian Lawler Collection)

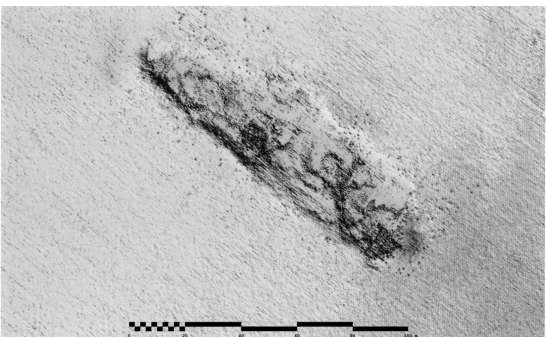

SS Manchester Engineer

This 4,302-ton, steamship of Manchester was owned by Manchester Liners Ltd and was built in Newcastle-upon-Tyne in 1902 by Northumberland S.B. Company Ltd. It was torpedoed without warning on 27th March 1916 by German submarine *U-44*; there was no loss of life. Lying NW/SE some 20km south of Tramore in County Waterford, the remains are relatively intact. At a general water depth of 61m, the wreck measures 109m x 15m and is c. 2m proud of the seabed. The RV *Celtic Voyager* surveyed the site in 2013. The black and white photo above shows the steamship under tow. (Ian Lawler Collection)

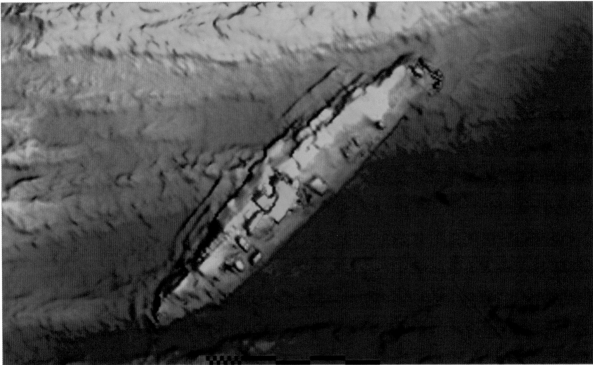

SS Miami

This 3,762-ton steamship of Glasgow was owned by Elders & Fyffes Ltd and built by Barclay, Curle & Company Ltd. Glasgow in 1904. It was torpedoed on 22nd June 1917 by German submarine *UC-51*, while en route from New York to Manchester with 3,700 tons of general cargo. There was no loss of life. The wreck is orientated NE/SW on the seafloor some 11km ESE of Fastnet and is relatively intact. At a general water depth of 64m, the wreck measures 108m x 22m and is c. 7m proud of the seabed. The RV *Celtic Voyager* surveyed the site in 2013. The black and white photo above shows the steamship discharging cargo. (Ian Lawler Collection)

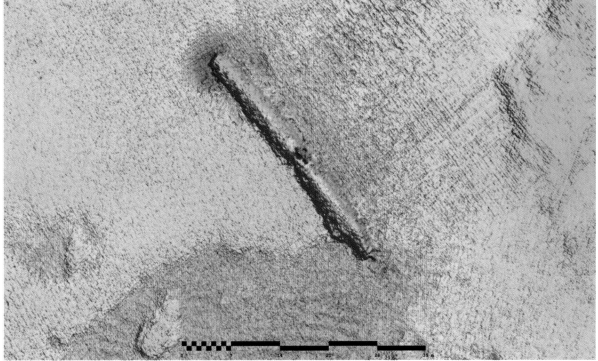

UC-42

The UC II class German minelayer U-boat was equipped with a deck gun, seven torpedoes and a total of 18 mines. The U-boat was lost during an attempt to lay mines across the mouth of Cork Harbour in September 1917 when a mine accidentally detonated resulting in the loss of the submarine and all 27 crew on board. Located 5km southeast of Roches Point, the *UC-42* is orientated NW/SE on the seabed and is relatively intact. It measures 36m x 5m and lies at a depth of 26m. It was originally discovered during a 2010 survey by INFOMAR; the RV *Keary* resurveyed the site in 2012. The black and white photo above labelled 'Going down to work on the *UC-42* off Queenstown, Ireland' shows a fully clad diver working on the wreck of the submarine shortly after it sank. (NH114630: Naval History and Heritage Command)

Imaging the RMS Lusitania

Surveying the Wreck Site

Various surveys of the RMS *Lusitania* have been carried out by both the Irish National Seabed Survey and INFOMAR since 2002. Multibeam imagery of the *Lusitania* has greatly advanced as the surveys were carried out, due to the increasing capabilities and higher ping rates of the various MBES systems used. On 26th March 2002 the first multibeam survey of the *Lusitania* was carried out by the SV *Bligh* as part of calibration tests for the newly installed EM1002S

multibeam system. Given the general water depth around the site of the *Lusitania* (93m) and the objectives of the surveys at the time (deepwater) the imagery produced was of a coarse nature yielding images of the wreck on the seafloor at c.3m resolution. Very little information can be taken from an image at this resolution regarding the state of the wreck but it does indicate accurate water depths at the site, the orientation of the wreck and the general state of the seafloor around it.

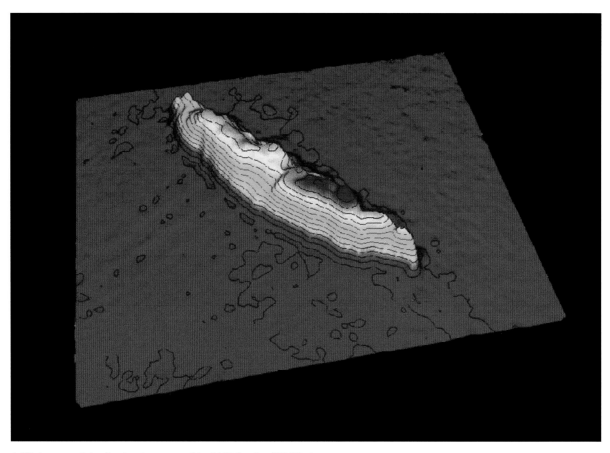

A 3D image of the *Lusitania* surveyed in 2002 by the SV *Bligh*.

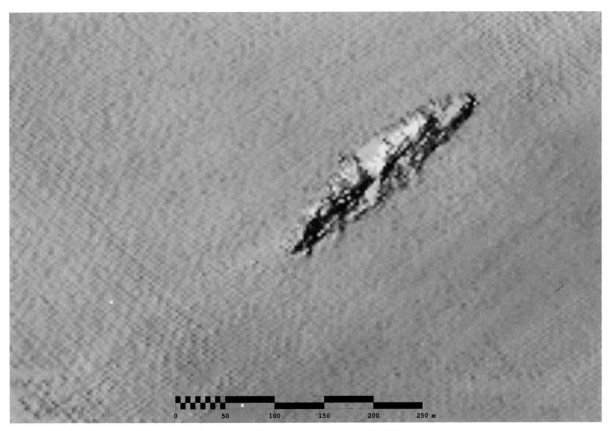

0   50   100   150   200   250 m

Plan view of the *Lusitania* as surveyed by the SV *Bligh* in 2002 using an EM1002S multibeam system.

A 3D image of the *Lusitania* acquired using an EM3002 system on board the RV *Keary* in 2009.

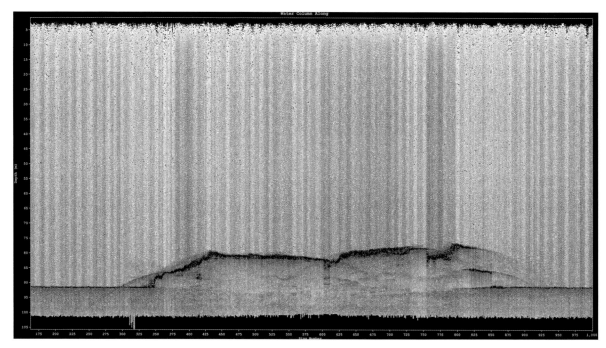

Water column profile view of the wreck of the *Lusitania* from the 2009 survey. The bow is on the left and the stern on the right.

Plan view of the *Lusitania* at a resolution of 25cm. The 2009 survey continued to yield greater detail than the earlier 2002 surveys.

In 2014 the RV *Celtic Voyager* conducted a survey using the high resolution EM2040 system. The additional detail can now be seen in this 25cm resolution version of the *Lusitania* in plan view. The wreck is orientated in a northeast–southwest direction and measures approximately 241m on the seafloor.

In 2009 the Geological Survey Ireland acquired the first of INFOMAR's shallow water survey fleet, the RV *Keary*. The RV *Keary* was fitted with an EM3002 multibeam system – a higher frequency high-performance shallow water system used for applications such as mapping of harbours, detection and mapping of underwater objects, and habitat mapping. In 2010 the RV *Keary* carried out a survey of the *Lusitania*. The imagery produced from this survey revealed in much greater detail the state of the wreck on the seafloor. Detail could now be clearly seen of the port side of the wreck (the *Lusitania* lies on its starboard side). The imagery produced was at a general resolution of 25–50cm which clearly showed the decay of the wreck which is slowly collapsing in on itself. In addition this multibeam system allowed for the collection of water column data along the track of the ship.

In 2013 the multibeam system used on the RV *Keary* was upgraded to the EM2040 system, which is of a similar specification to the previous system used but with the addition of advanced features of deepwater mapping for near-bottom environments. The EM2040 system has allowed similar resolution imagery and mapping to be created, but of much higher quality. In July 2013 the RV *Keary* conducted a survey of the *Lusitania* while on transit to Dingle Bay. The new imagery created from this survey (at 25cm resolution) provided a visual of the wreck in even greater detail than was possible with the survey in 2010. Evidence of the wreck collapsing in on itself is visible on the stern end. A cross-section of the 3D image produced shows this feature of the wreck. The area of upperworks collapsed onto the seabed, including the funnels, fixings and deck furniture from the navigation and A decks, is now also visible in much greater detail.

The EM2040 system was also installed on the RV *Celtic Voyager* in early 2014. While finalising the Southern Priority Area Block in September 2014, the RV *Celtic Voyager* carried out a full site survey of the

A 3D view of the survey data acquired in 2014. The wreck can be seen lying on her starboard side with a significant break in the bottom of the hull also visible. The wreck lies at a general depth of between 87m and 93m and rises between 9m and 12m off the seafloor.

Lusitania. This included the wreck itself and the area surrounding the wreck which is charted as a 'Historic Wreck' site indicating that it is protected from any unauthorised interference. The designated protected area is 4.5km x 7.5km in extent. The conditions at the time of survey were favourable resulting in state-of-the-art, high-quality multibeam images and water column data not previously seen.

Most Recent Imagery of the Wreck

This new sonar imagery of the *Lusitania* is the most detailed information and overview of the wreck site compiled to date. Analysis of the sonar data is providing new insights into the wreck and gives a solid framework upon which new research and analysis can be based. The multibeam imagery not only provides a

sense of the scale and nature of the site, but is also a tangible connection to the wreck and to the dramatic and tragic events that surrounded the liner's sinking. The wreck is clearly defined on the sea floor. It lies on its starboard side and measures 241m in length by 46m in width and 14.7m in maximum height, standing on average 9.9m off the seabed. The vessel is orientated NE–SW on the seafloor, with its bow to the north-east. Lying as it does on its starboard side, the area where the torpedo struck the vessel is concealed. A large debris field lies along the starboard side of the wreck indicative of where parts of the superstructure, funnels, etc. have collapsed onto the seafloor. Traces of the smoke stacks and steam pipes are also visible in the debris zone. The violent nature of its sinking, several salvage operations and man-made interventions, depth charging by the Royal Navy in the late 1940s, the

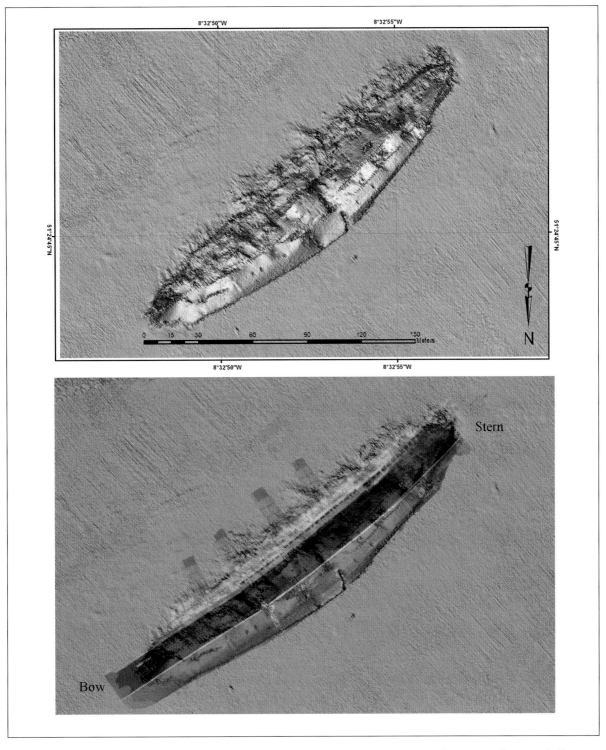

Comparative views of the wreck with the top image showing the multibeam view of the *Lusitania* as it currently lies on the seabed today. The multibeam imagery of the wreck in the bottom picture has been overlaid with an image of the great liner as it was originally. The overlay image attempts to help understand how the wreck of the liner is currently lying on the seabed and how it has disintegrated over time. A comparison of both images highlights many features on the port side of the vessel, including portholes, funnel outlines and individual sections of steel hull. Though collapsed in places, the wreck remains relatively intact on the seabed with a substantial debris field around it where upper works have collapsed onto the sea floor. The imagery provides a sense of the scale and history of the site.

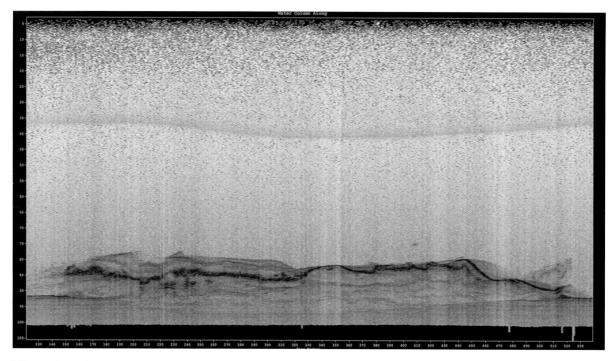

Water column imagery across track of the *Lusitania* from the EM2040 system – bow to stern – left to right.

natural decaying processes and the ravages of the North Atlantic swell have all taken their toll on the remains of the vessel. The imagery shows that, although slowly collapsing, the bow is still standing proud of the seabed with many structural elements clearly discernible. However, many of the bulkheads and decks have collapsed and the hull is separated from the bulkheads in many places.

Many features on the port side of the vessel are similarly clearly discernible in the sonar imagery,

including the passenger and cargo door openings, portholes and individual sections of steel hull plating. Much new information can be gleaned from this data including information on the areas most severely damaged at the time of its sinking, such as the impact to the bow when it hit the seabed. Further impacts can be seen amidships where a large tear ripped through the hull when the liner broke its back after crashing into the seafloor. Various holes or tears are imaged, both on the hull and along the deck areas.

Opposite: Cover of a musical score composed in memory of those lost on the *Lusitania*. (Ian Lawler Collection)

"The archaeological investigation of deepwater shipwrecks is advancing all the time and extensive work has been carried out in recent years on some of the deepest wrecks yet discovered."

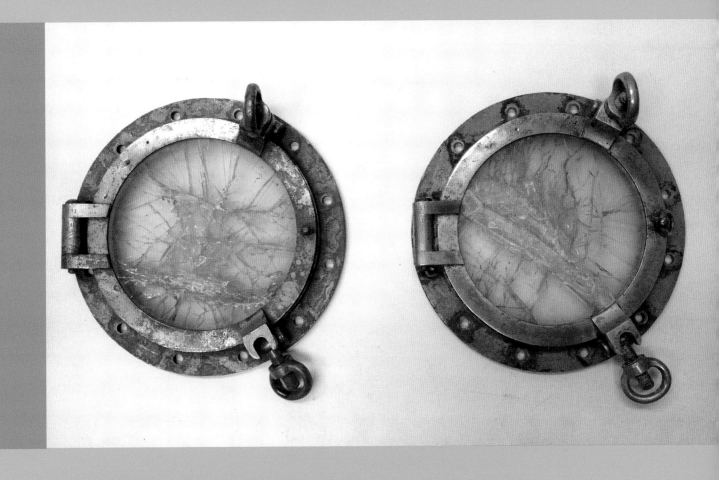

The Archaeology of a Deepwater Shipwreck

Deepwater Shipwrecks and Archaeological Investigations

No comprehensive archaeological study of the RMS *Lusitania* has been undertaken to date. The role of Government managers in the protection of our underwater cultural heritage does not necessarily provide for pure research on any specific site. Given the constraints that exist in relation to resources, scale and nature of work briefs and in particular with sites such as the *Lusitania* (where depth limits prohibit general diving) there has been no opportunity for the National Monuments Service to focus archaeological attention on the wreck beyond what has been done under conditions pertaining to dive licences issued to third parties. Licence conditions normally require copies of surveys, video and photographic records as well as individual diver reports to be submitted to the National Monuments Service. There they are placed on the licence file and copied to the archive of the Wreck Inventory of Ireland Database, which is maintained by the National Monuments Service. In this way, information is obtained which is then accessible to the general public and researchers. While the majority of reports reflect visual impressions from sports divers with no archaeological requirements, such information can contribute valuable additions to our knowledge of the wreck site, including its condition, rate of deterioration, collapse, exposed objects, overburdens of sand and silt, scouring and netting. Where more extensive investigation is being proposed on the wreck site, with more expansive research agendas, like that of the 2011 expedition to the site by its owner F. Gregg Bemis and National Geographic,

then more clearly defined method statements and archaeological input is required as a condition of any licence issued. In this way best archaeological practice is applied.

The archaeological investigation of deepwater shipwrecks is advancing all the time and extensive work has been carried out in recent years on some of the deepest wrecks yet discovered. With advances in technology and improvements in surveying techniques developed specifically for archaeological purposes, access to wrecks at greater depths is now fully achievable and archaeological investigation to the highest international standards possible. *Lusitania*, however, awaits such scientific investigation. The work of Robert Ballard in 1993 and the project carried out by National Geographic in 2011 included provision for assessing the wreck site from a cultural heritage perspective, and both addressed some of the archaeological questions relating to the wreck itself, its sinking and site formation processes. A definitive archaeological appraisal, however, has yet to be undertaken.

Any deepwater investigation, whether focused purely on mapping the site remotely or physically placing divers on the wreck, is expensive and logistically challenging. Lying at 93+m in the open Atlantic Ocean, subject to adverse weather conditions, strong tidal variations and cold, dark water, any activity focused on the site of the *Lusitania* requires extensive pre-planning, inclusive consultation, cohesive mobilisation and on-site team working. In addition, a favourable weather window is critical for the success of any expedition to the wreck site. As with all deeply submerged shipwrecks, there are preparatory and

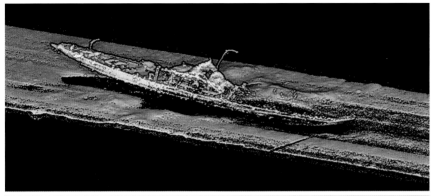

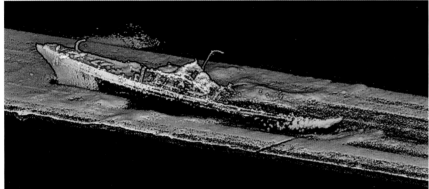

3D image of the wreck of the steam yacht *Anona*, lost in 1944 , which lies in over 4,000 feet of water in the Viosca Knoll in the Gulf of Mexico. The grey data is high-res multibeam (Kongsberg EM 2040 400 kHz system, mounted on C&C Technologies' *C-Surveyor* VI AUV). The blue data is from the Blue View 5000 3D sonar scanner mounted on the DSSI *Global Explorer* ROV. (Image by C&C Technologies and courtesy of BOEM; http://www.boem.gov/)

operational challenges when considering any investigation, and the wreck of the *Lusitania* is no different. This is borne out by technical diver descriptions of what is needed to prepare for diving on the wreck and the actuality of the diving itself (see contributions by Stewart Andrews and Pat Coughlan pp 86–87). In the case of any large-scale research project, the logistical implications increase exponentially. Comparable operational requirements were applied in the past to salvage work at the site, but the delicacy required and dedication to detail that is fundamental to archaeological investigation underscores the need to apply best practice. Archaeological methods are now being applied through the use of advanced technology to deepwater shipwreck investigation and are fast becoming accepted best practice for survey, recording and excavation of "deep-submergence archaeology" (Wachsmann 2011, 208–217). Perhaps this approach is best encapsulated by Brendan Foley, Chief Scientist with the United States' National Oceanic and Atmospheric Administration's *Ocean Explorer*, when writing about deepwater archaeology. The term 'deepwater', he

wrote, had very little to do with actual depth but instead deepwater is viewed "in terms of technology and methods necessary to access those depths. The use of robotic systems, *in situ* sensors, precision navigation and rigorous, technology-intensive survey methods are what sets deepwater archaeology apart from its shallow water cousin" (Foley 2010). Any investigation of the wreck site of the *Lusitania* will need to apply similar technology to ensure archaeologically sound results.

Current publications have increasingly emphasised this approach to deepwater shipwreck archaeology (Bingham *et al*. 2010; Warren *et al*. 2007), further highlighting the need for collaborative and interdisciplinary methodologies to be applied when undertaking such work (Church & Warren 2009; Damour 2013). This is perhaps best illustrated by the recent impressive work carried out on some much deeper wreck sites than that of the *Lusitania*. In the Gulf of Mexico, for example, the Bureau of Ocean Energy Management (as part of its Deep Wrecks Project) has successfully surveyed, investigated and archaeologically excavated a number of wrecks in waters as deep as 4,000 feet (1219m) (www.boem.gov).

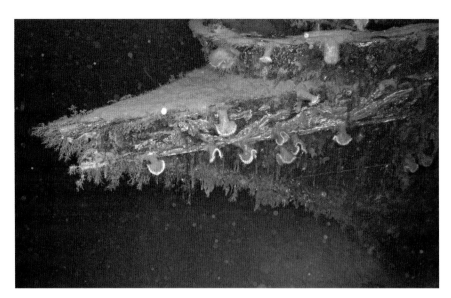

Bow of the *Anona* showing biological growth. Shipwrecks like this serve as artificial reefs in the deep ocean. (Image by DSSI *Global Explorer* ROV. March 2014 and courtesy of BOEM; http://www.boem.gov/

The remains of the eighteenth-century *Nuestra Señora de las Mercedes*, located off the coast of southern Spain at a depth of over 1,000 feet (305m), is the focus of ongoing work by the Spanish National Museum of Underwater Archaeology (Negueruela Martínez *et al*. 2015). Other wrecks in waters comparable to that of the *Lusitania* continue to be surveyed and researched, such as the early eighteenth-century Ormen Lange shipwreck located some 120km north-west of Kristiansund in central Norway (Skoglund 2015), and the much earlier but strikingly well-preserved wreck site at a depth of 125m in the Baltic Sea, generically referred to as the 'Ghost Ship' (Dixelius *et al*. 2011). The latter wreck can be reached by means of technical and saturation diving as well as the use of deepwater technology in much the same way as might be applied to the scientific investigation of the wreck of the *Lusitania*.

Cost is a serious issue when considering work on deepwater wrecks and one that needs to be realistically factored into any project. Such preparatory work should include consideration of the financial and logistical elements that need to be put in place to ensure that the investigative work can be carried out to the highest standards in terms of safety, diving and, in the case of historic wreck sites such as that of the *Lusitania*, the application of archaeological best practice, to include pre-disturbance assessment, on-site recording, post-excavation conservation, report writing and publication. A less rigorous approach would effectively amount to traditional salvage which has no place in the investigation of a wreck of this importance. A multidisciplinary and interdisciplinary approach is therefore essential for ensuring that a knowledge-based method is applied while also factoring in the sharing of costs, logistical expertise and resources.

The recent work of the Geological Survey Ireland seabed mapping programme is proving essential to our understanding of the current condition of the wreck and will help inform any future proposed projects on the wreck and the State's consideration of such proposals. Such mapping is an essential first step in any management strategy for a site, informing preliminary site investigation planning while providing insights into the orientation of the wreck, the general site conditions and the wider site or debris field beyond the main part of the wreck itself. The seabed mapping imagery provides an overview of the entire site which, because of the sheer scale of the wreck site of the *Lusitania*, cannot be achieved by individual divers, archaeologists or even by deepwater ROVs, AUVs (autonomous underwater vehicles), etc. The imagery provides the initial macro-view that gives context to the micro-views of individual parts of the wreck that are achievable during any given dive project. This is not a new approach (Church & Warren 2008, 103–104) but it is one that is improving all the time, with greater quality imaging, higher resolution and new ways of mapping.

Advances and refinements in recording and surveying techniques are equally important. For example, accurate acoustic position fixing and short or long baseline mapping techniques are essential when considering the recovery of artefactual material from wrecks at depth. The use of such locational data enables the development of a concise distribution model and full observational understanding of a deepwater site. As mooted by Warren (2016, 248), if these techniques are not integral to the overall archaeological mapping strategy for the exploration of a deepwater shipwreck, "little more than pretty site pictures with only limited scientific value" is achieved.

Deterioration Studies on Deepwater Shipwrecks

A cohesive scientific study of the deterioration and corrosion effects on the structural integrity of the wreck of the *Lusitania* also needs to be done. Reports in the recent past have suggested that the wreck is collapsing at a rapid and "alarming" rate (Tolson 2010, 150; Stolley 2014). It is obvious that, inevitably, there has been collapse of internal structures over time, originally initiated by the impact of the explosions before the ship sank, followed by the impact when it hit the seabed and came to rest on the seafloor. Since then less robust internal supports have also clearly given way causing parts of the superstructure to collapse inward and downward over time. Reports of both the Royal Navy and Irish Naval Service depth charging the wreck in the 1940s and 1950s, though unverified, may also have led to damage and destabilisation, as would the unmonitored salvage works carried out on the wreck by Oceaneering International Inc. in 1982.

When built, the *Lusitania* stood to a height of 18.3m to the upper boat deck or top of the bow railing. Today the wreck sits some 14m off the seabed at its bow end. Along the main body of the wreck at mid-ships it is lower due to collapse that occurred when the ship broke during the sinking, and subsequent deterioration has also taken place due to the fact that the shipwreck lies on its starboard side, with the full weight of the bulk of the structure

pressing down on itself. While this is not a scientific statement on deterioration, the fact that 14m of the wreck is still proud of the seabed and that it is still clearly recognisable as the remains of a substantial ship even after 100 years on the seabed, indicate that the wreck is not deteriorating to the extent that recent media reports suggest but is gradually collapsing over time, as would be expected of any steel and iron structure at that depth on the seabed. This is inevitable. Indeed the results of INFOMAR's recent mapping of the wreck site clearly show the areas of damage and collapse and are helping to inform more accurately on the deterioration of the site. Structural breaks and cracks have become apparent. Sections of hull collapse and fragmented wreckage on the seabed to the immediate starboard side where the funnels and other hull appurtenances have collapsed onto the seabed are also visible. While a certain amount of collapse is occurring on an ongoing and perhaps incremental basis the nature and extent of this collapse remain scientifically unquantified.

Other factors may contribute to loss of structural integrity and damage to the wreck. Recent studies on corrosion, exposure to hydrocarbons, microbiology and other environmental factors affecting metal shipwrecks on some of the Gulf of Mexico deepwater wreck sites suggest that the deterioration of a metal wreck is a complex process and subject to multiple factors. Funding was made available to the GOM-SCHEMA project to investigate the impacts of the 2010 *Deepwater Horizon* oil spill on deepwater historic shipwrecks. It also analysed corrosion and hydrocarbon exposure and sought to assess microbiological and archaeological aspects of the sites affected. Variation in rates of corrosion is primarily determined by oxygen availability, which affects the viability of marine micro-organisms on any metal or iron surface or within corrosion layers and the underlying metal surfaces (www.boem.gov/GOM-SCHEMA/). Corrosion studies elsewhere, ongoing now for a number of decades, have again confirmed that the reduction of dissolved oxygen is the primary process determining the overall rate of corrosion (MacLeod 2002, 698). Corrosion studies aimed at initiating corrosion on various metals and creating deterioration models can generate lifetime predictive data for a given wreck (MacLeod 2013, 474). Management and protection strategies are thereby informed by the ongoing site and wreck-formation processes, which in turn facilitate consideration of what may be appropriate in any investigation of an individual wreck site.

Such is the volume of fish life at the wreck of the *Lusitania* at times, that it has been targeted by trawl fishermen, the evidence for which is often left on the wreck in the form of tattered nets and fishing tackle that has become snagged. While such activity is prohibited and should not occur within the designated exclusion zone, policing it remains difficult. Close collaboration between the National Monuments Service, the Irish Naval Service and the Receiver of Wreck (Customs and Excise) facilitates monitoring of the wreck site and the general policing requirements for the site. Marine Notices have been issued by the Department of Transport, Tourism and Sport highlighting the protected nature of the wreck and the exclusion zone around it, but at times they have been ignored. Such trawling activity can impact the wreck, with nets pulling and tugging on its structure, having obvious negative consequences. No evidence for extensive trawling has been identified, however, and it

appears that the snagged and torn remains of nets on the wreck reflect opportunistic fishing by individual fishermen or accidental snagging of nets rather than a concerted effort to regularly trawl the wreck as a fishing site.

The potential negative effect of cultural tourism on protected wreck sites also needs to be assessed. The protected wreck of the SS *Yongala* is relevant here. A luxury iron-hulled passenger liner, built in 1903, the ship foundered and sank in Cape Bowling Green Bay off Queensland, Australia in 1911. Though in much shallower water (its bow is at 19.6m), the *Yongala's* distance from shore (12 nautical miles) and exposed nature provide several elements for comparison to the *Lusitania*, not least the general site conditions whereby it is exposed fully to all weather conditions (Viduka 2007, 3–7). The study of diver activity indicated negative impacts on the wreck site. While natural events such as storms and cyclones had their obvious deleterious effects on the wreck site, ill-considered mooring by dive operators over the site and opportunistic interference by individual divers also resulted in serious negative impacts on the wreck. This impact was not just to the cultural heritage but also to the natural ecosystem that had evolved at the wreck

The *Lusitania's* telltale recovered by Eoin McGarry following the 2011 National Geographic expedition, before conservation. (Courtesy of Laurence Dunne Archaeology)

The *Lusitania's* telltale after undergoing conservation. (Courtesy of Laurence Dunne Archaeology)

site since its sinking, with the result that the wreck is now supporting an astonishing multiplicity of marine flora and fauna (*ibid.*, 62). Management strategies applied to the wreck of the *Lusitania*, when assessing any proposed diving expedition, involve strict conditions on how mooring is carried out, require that archaeological monitoring of dive operations by officers of the National Monuments Service be accommodated in so far as deemed necessary and seek to ensure the least impact occurs to the wreck in terms of its natural and cultural environment.

Artefact Recovery and Conservation Strategies

In 2011, as part of the licensed National Geographic expedition to the wreck site, both the National Museum of Ireland and the National Monuments Service agreed that a select number of artefacts could be recovered and specific conditions in this regard were added to the licence issued to the wreck's owner, Mr F. Gregg Bemis. A detailed recovery strategy, overseen by professional archaeologists and a conservation strategy, supervised by a professional conservator and approved by the National Museum of

Ireland, formed part of this agreement. The artefacts recovered consisted of a telemotor, a telltale and four portholes. Part of the agreed recovery methodologies included the use of Ultra Short Base Line position mapping to record the location of the artefacts prior to recovery, supported by photographic and video recording and generation of a site distribution map.

Overview of Artefacts Recovered
Laurence Dunne

All artefacts identified for recovery no longer formed part of the coherent wreck structure, but lay as individual objects on the seabed or within the wreck and therefore did not necessitate any excavation of silts or impact on the wreck itself. The services of two archaeologists, Ms Julianna O'Donoghue and the author were engaged by Mr Bemis to provide the maritime and underwater archaeological expertise for the project. The informed agreed archaeological methodology for the pre-distrubance survey, the actual recovery of the artefacts and the conservation strategy thereafter, were then implemented. Once recovered, the project archaeologists and professional conservator Ian Panter, of York Archaeological Trust Conservation

The *Lusitania*'s telemotor before and after the conservation process. The telemotor was located on the ship's bridge and formed part of the ship's steering mechanism. (Courtesy of Laurence Dunne Archaeology)

Laboratory, who was also present to advise on handling, immediate conservation requirements and temporary storage, immediately attended to the artefacts.

The main dive team, led by Waterford-based diver Eoin McGarry, following the agreed recovery methodology, secured the artefacts on the seabed and oversaw the successful, controlled recovery of each one from the wreck site, whilst maintaining close communication with the project archaeologists during the recovery operation. Once on board the dive vessel, rapid first aid took place, including photography and video recording, artefact tagging and wrapping and then the careful placement in temporary storage tanks. The artefacts were subsequently fully conserved by Dr Ian Panter and the author, under a licence to alter issued by the National Museum of Ireland (Dunne, 2013, 8–9).

Telltale telegraph

A drum-shaped telltale telegraph was the first artefact recovered. The telltale was a supplementary dial instrument electrically connected to the turbine of the ship and features a single pointer that denotes the direction of the engine and would have been located on the bridge. The one recovered is inscribed with the words AHEAD and ASTERN on its outer rim face. Tiny fragments of the original 3mm white glass from its dial face still remain in the glazing groove and cleaning during the conservation process revealed a number of interesting features including the manufacturer's name, *Chadburn of Liverpool*, who were the world's foremost designers and makers of ships telegraphs and other instruments at that time.

Telemotor

The telemotor is a complex, upright pedestal type piece of equipment directly linked to the steering of the vessel. Two telemotors were fitted in the wheelhouse of the *Lusitania* at the rear of the navigation bridge. A third telemotor was located in the aft steering station on the boat deck under the docking bridge. The recovered bridge telemotor is a Brown's Patent type although interestingly no manufacturer's name was found during conservation. A serial number,

A543-8, was revealed on the side edge of the uppermost horizontal circular closing plate.

Interestingly, there are two repair brazes on the telemotor, the most obvious of which is to the casing through which the shaft is attached. The second braze is to the underside of the gear case. The conservation of the telemotor was difficult due to its complex and often awkward array of components but successfully revealed, even after 100 years, the quality of the instrument and excellence of manufacture.

First-class portholes

Two large sub-rectangular first-class cabin vented windows were recovered, one of which was badly damaged. However, the second window is virtually intact and still opens freely. The windows feature a distinctive Regency-style openwork pattern on the exterior face of their vents at the top. The motif comprises a central roundel in a multi-foil marigold pattern from which vegetative scrollwork extends to left and right. These vents are mechanically opened or closed by a hand-operated knurled knob situated on the interior bottom right-hand side. Internally these windows opened and closed with a finger pull and twist locking bolt. These large vented portholes also feature an external, heavy duty bolt-locking mechanism that can only be opened and closed by a member of the crew with a master key into a central square key socket (3D representation: www.ldarch.ie).

Both windows are hinged on the right, indicating that they are from the starboard side of the forward area of the boat deck. Of particular historical interest are photographs of the forward starboard boat deck taken from one of the 150-ton cranes at the shipyard on the Clyde when the *Lusitania* was being fitted out before her sea trials. Several other photographs were taken of the boat deck area during voyages that clearly show these distinctive vented windows.

Circular portholes

Two circular brass portholes that are identical in form and size were also recovered. The portholes opened inwards but when closed, the porthole was made watertight by a rubber seal that extended around the inside of the sash. Much of the rubber seal has survived in both portholes. The two portholes are double stamped onto the sash and frame sections of the hinge with the numbers 741 and 745 respectively. The similarity of the numbers and the fact that they were recovered in very close proximity to each other and to the telegraphic instruments from the bridge strongly suggest that they were most likely from the bridge itself or from the shelter deck area.

The archaeological recovery and conservation of these artefacts allow us a window into the workings of the *Lusitania* – the mechanisms that steered the ship, and the portals that adorned the sides of the vessel during its lifetime on the seas, perhaps opened and shut by many who lost their lives during the sinking. The excellent preservation of each one is testament to the quality of craftsmanship employed in their

One of two round portholes recovered from the *Lusitania* by Eoin McGarry in 2011 following the National Geographic expedition, prior to conservation. (Courtesy of Laurence Dunne Archaeology)

The two round portholes after undergoing conservation. (Courtesy of Laurence Dunne Archaeology)

manufacture. By engaging the expertise to oversee the successful archaeological recovery, recording and professional conservation of such significant objects, we ensure that they remain as a tangible link to the ship itself and the majesty of a once great liner.

A Living Site – When Nature Takes Over

Shipwrecks can become living sites. The pervading impression and frequent allure of some wrecks – not least the *Lusitania* – is that they are sites of loss, tragedy, death and burial while often being at the centre of historic controversies. While all of the above is undoubtedly true and due regard on that level should be given, a site like the *Lusitania* can also become a living sanctuary in its own right. Nature can and will invariably take over and a shipwreck will attract a variety of marine life, becoming an organic entity completely removed from its original purpose. Some sites become living reefs, others the focus of passing shoals of migrating fish life. Invariably the superstructure will attract and be colonised by marine growth. Such faunal exploitation will be determined by temperature, depth and quality of the water together with tidal conditions at the site, but once nature takes hold these historic wreck sites can often begin to reveal more about the natural world than they can about past tragedies, conflicts, sinking events or the human stories of those on board. The site, therefore, takes on a secondary but no less important value as a reserve for marine flora and fauna, becoming a living entity on the seabed.

Although it is clear from accounts by individual divers and from photographic and video evidence that the wreck plays host to a variety of marine organisms, the nature and extent of marine life on the *Lusitania* have yet to be scientifically studied. Many shipwrecks around the world have become sites of natural interest, often within the context of a marine sanctuary where the wreck becomes part of a much wider submerged ecological landscape and is appreciated on that level, rather than for its specific cultural interest. The *Lusitania* has yet to be considered in this way and perhaps the historical drama that surrounds the story

of the ship and wreck itself has curtailed awareness of the need for scientific study into the natural changes and systems forming on the wreck site. The wreck clearly presents an opportunity for study of the marine organisms that have colonised it over the years and for the resultant positive visual experience that this multiplicity of marine life can provide for those diving and viewing the wreck site. Understanding how the natural, living heritage on one of the world's most enigmatic wreck sites is contributing to our marine ecosystem can add fresh interest in the site, with the marine life as the focus of attention while the wreck itself in that context is secondary but still central to the whole experience.

Marine micro-organisms and associated processes can also be destructive. Researchers looking at the wreck of the RMS *Titanic* over the last two decades have shown that, apart from being a vibrant underwater habitat, one of the species the site supports is a bacterium, *Halomonas Titanicae*, named after the ship itself. The bacteria live inside the icicle-like growths of rust, generically referred to as 'rusticles' and essentially they devour the iron fabric of the hull. In turn they recycle nutrients from this consuming action back into the ocean ecosystem. While this is a natural process, it is accelerating the destruction of the wreck of the *Titanic* (Cullimore & Johnston, 2003). The degree to which, if any, similar activity is occurring on the remains of the *Lusitania* is not known but it is only by looking at the wreck as a living organism that we can begin to build a whole new dataset of important information on it which, in turn, may lead to a complete reinterpretation of the wreck site from both a natural and conservation perspective. While the historical and archaeological significance of the wreck site is well established, the wreck of the *Lusitania* may also need to be considered as a living habitat that is now contributing as much to our appreciation of the ocean world as the history and stories of the ship itself have done to connect us with our past.

Managing & Protecting the Wreck Site

The Legislative Basis and Legal Background

Since 1995 the wreck of the *Lusitania* has been protected by an Underwater Heritage Order which has defined a zone of exclusion around the wreck site measuring five nautical miles by two, and within which a range of activities specified in the legislation (section 3 (3) of the National Monuments (Amendment) Act 1987) as well as any damage to the wreck are deemed unlawful unless done under a licence granted under section 3 of that Act. The exclusion zone was put in place to ensure that not only is the wreck itself protected, but the area around it – which includes the debris field that formed when the ship broke up on its

way to the bottom and which has continued to expand in the general vicinity over the subsequent years – is equally protected. The *Lusitania* is the only maritime site to date to have been considered sufficiently important in national and international terms to be afforded protection by an Underwater Heritage Order. As it is now over over a century old all provisions of the Act protecting wrecks over 100 years old apply. Not only the wreck but all of the archaeological objects contained within and around it are also included under the terms of the Order. All material therefore on the site of the *Lusitania*, not simply the wreck and its appurtenances, which are in private ownership, but the thousands of other personal items associated with those on board or any cargo are protected. Likewise,

Irish Naval Service ship during one of its many patrols over the wreck of the RMS *Lusitania*. (Photo Karl Brady)

Lifebuoy from the RMS *Lusitania* currently on display in the National Museum of Ireland, Collins Barracks. The lifebuoy was picked up by a passing trawler 72 miles off the Fastnet Lighthouse a few weeks after the sinking. (National Museum of Ireland)

while the extent of the ownership rights of Mr Bemis are clearly understood and acknowledged, all licence applications made to the State to carry out diving or other forms of exploratory activity on the wreck site, including the recovery of artefacts, are given due consideration and responded to in accordance with the provisions of the National Monuments Act and in keeping with both national and international archaeological best practice (Moore 2015, 16–19).

Judicial review proceedings relating to regulation of activities on the wreck of the Lusitania

Seán Kirwan

The legal implications of the making of the Underwater Heritage Order in terms of regulation of diving and other activities on the wreck were considered by the Courts between 2005 and 2007. The case also looked at the question of how the general law on regulation of archaeological excavation applied to intrusive investigation of the wreck.

What follows here sets out in broad terms the scope and outcome of those proceedings, which were initiated by the owner of the wreck (Mr F. Gregg Bemis) to challenge by way of judicial review a decision made by the Minister for Arts, Heritage, Gaeltacht and the Islands, Síle de Valera, T.D. in 2001 in respect of a licence application. This is not a legal interpretation nor is it intended as a full analysis of those proceedings. In general terms, 'judicial review' can be characterised as a process whereby persons can ask the High Court to examine the legal soundness of administrative decisions (e.g. decisions in respect of licence applications). Again, in broad terms, its focus is the procedural process whereby decisions were arrived at rather than the substantive merits of a decision.

The wreck having become subject to an Underwater Heritage Order, as earlier explained, the carrying out of any activities set out in section 3 of the National Monuments (Amendment) Act 1987 became subject to a licensing requirement under that section. The activities set out in section 3 include both diving without interfering with the wreck and activities which do result in damage having an impact on the wreck. Also, any activity in any location within the State, being an activity which comes within the scope of section 26 of the National Monuments Act 1930 (as amended), is subject to a licensing requirement under section 26. The activities covered by section 26 are what would be generally referred to as archaeological excavation. Importantly, the 1987 Act had amended the definition of 'land' for the purposes of the National Monuments Acts to include land covered by water.

In early 2001 an application was made by Mr Bemis under section 3 of the 1987 Act to carry out investigations of the wreck which would involve interference with it. The only form available for use in applying for a licence under section 3 was for non-intrusive diving, and the applicant had used this but modified it. The precise meaning of the letter issued on behalf of the Minister in response was in issue in the proceedings; the Supreme Court (*Bemis v. Minister for Arts, Heritage, Gaeltacht and the Islands and Ors.* 27th March 2007 (SC) IESC 10) saw it as saying that the application was invalid. Further, the Supreme Court saw the Minister as either misunderstanding the scope of section 3 (i.e. seeing it as restricted to non-intrusive diving), which was an error in law, or acting unreasonably in deciding that the only form of application for intrusive investigation she would consider was an application for non-intrusive diving under section 3 of the 1987 Act coupled with an application for a section 26 licence under the 1930 Act. On that basis it upheld the finding of the High Court that the Minister had acted *ultra vires* (i.e. beyond her powers) in rejecting the application. However, these grounds were narrower than the findings of the High Court, which had, in particular, found the Minister to have been wrong in considering that the work proposed in the 2001 application came within the scope of archaeological excavation as regulated by section 26 of the 1930 Act. The Supreme Court (Macken J.) stated, in contrast, "The Minister is and was entitled to contend that what was proposed by the Respondent as set out in his application of April 2001 required him to apply for a licence pursuant to Section 26 of the Act of 1930. The works, prima facie, are capable of falling within the ambit of this section and are therefore not permitted without such a licence. It is not necessary to go beyond the ordinary meaning of the above words to reach such a conclusion. Any work proposed which comes within the ordinary meaning of 'digging' or of 'excavation' engages the section, once it is the case that an object or structure of archaeological interest, such as items in or around the wreck of the Lusitania or even the Lusitania itself, lie in or under or partly under land beneath the sea, and once the purpose of the dig or excavation is known". Indeed, a key finding of general application coming out of the litigation is that licensing requirements under section 3 of the 1987 Act and section 26 of the 1930 Act are freestanding and that one does not exclude the other; where a proposed activity comes within the scope of both sections then both forms of licence are necessary.

The Supreme Court's acceptance of the archaeological interest of objects in or around the wreck, and even of the wreck itself, is also clear, though perhaps not addressed in as detailed a manner as the High Court (*Bemis v. Minister for Arts, Heritage, Gaeltacht and the Islands and Ors.* 17th June 2005 (HC) IESC 207) which had referred to the archaeological interest attaching to the wreck due to its belonging to a past society, as well as to its coming within the definition

of 'archaeological object' under the National Monuments on grounds of its association with an Irish historical event (the High Court acknowledging the First World War to be such an event).

The High Court had, in addition to addressing those findings strictly necessary to determine the case before it, gone on to address a range of issues raised in the proceedings in regard to the weight to be attached by the Minister to the owner's property interests in the wreck when the Minister came to decide on licence applications made by the owner. In broad terms, the High Court considered that insufficient regard had been given to these. The Supreme Court considered that no ruling should be made on these points, as they were unnecessary to determine the case, and stated that the findings made by the High Court on these matters were not to be considered binding. The Supreme Court did, however, give some pointers for future cases by stating (Macken J.) "it is sufficient to state on this topic that there is ample case law on the correct exercise by a Minister of his statutory powers in the case of the private property of an individual, when balancing any right to a licence in respect of the same against the interests of the State in protecting, maintaining or controlling the use of that property, for the common good".

It is important to note that while certain issues (as outlined above) did result in litigation between the owner of the wreck and the Minister, the existence of the Underwater Heritage Order has not prevented diving. Throughout the period since the making of the Order in 1995, licences have regularly been granted to the owner, his agents or other interested parties to undertake investigations that might shed light on some of the questions that remain in relation to the circumstances that gave rise to the *Lusitania*'s rapid sinking or might add to our understanding of the wreck itself and its general condition on the seabed.

Memorandum of Understanding between Mr Bemis and the National Monuments Service

In April 2013 the National Monuments Service agreed a Memorandum of Understanding with Mr Bemis "in regard to present and future research priorities for the protected wreck". The Memorandum sets out the broad agenda for future research on the wreck, identifies areas where there may be room for collaboration on projects and clearly defines the respective position of all stakeholders so that there is a clear understanding of their objectives and legal obligations.

The overall intention of the Memorandum is to try to facilitate Mr Bemis' legitimate research interests while also protecting the wreck site and the artefacts contained within it or in its immediate vicinity. It does not replace or supplant the normal licensing requirements. Although there are points of difference in relation to the way one might approach the protection and investigation of the wreck, all discussion in relation to licensing requirements is undertaken with respect to the spirit of the Memorandum.

The Lusitania and the National Museum of Ireland
Nessa O'Connor

Since 1994, the National Museum of Ireland has had a continuous involvement with issues relating to the wreck of the Lusitania and proposals to dive on the site. These reviews were carried out in conjunction with colleagues in the Underwater Archaeology Unit of the National Monuments Service. This has been the case because of the statutory role of the Director of the National Museum of Ireland in respect of archaeological objects, as provided in the National Monuments Acts 1930 to 2004 and in the Merchant Shipping (Salvage and Wreck) Act, 1993.
It is noteworthy that the definition of 'archaeological object' in the National Monuments Acts is broad and is not in any way date confined. Instead,

A lifeboat oar, branded 'Lusitania' recovered from the water off the Clare coast about three months after the disaster. (National Museum of Ireland)

archaeological objects are defined in terms of intrinsic value that is substantially enhanced by either their archaeological interest or association with an Irish historical event or person.

In late 1994, the National Museum of Ireland and other State agencies became aware of increased diving activity in the vicinity of the wreck of the Lusitania. A series of reports appeared in The Sunday Press that suggested that rival dive teams were attempting to locate art cargo and other personal property on board the vessel, to the detriment of this important historic wreck and its contents (Maas 1995). Early that year and partly as a consequence, an Underwater Heritage Order was placed on the wreck and the immediate area around it. This was due to the risk presented by the activities of groups of unauthorised divers. The National Museum had a role at that time, in advising the Minister for Arts, Culture and the Gaeltacht and in endeavouring to ensure the protection of the site in the face of this increasing risk of damage and potential loss to its historic structure and content.

On 25th January 1995 the then Minister for Arts, Culture and the Gaeltacht, Michael D. Higgins, stated in answer to Dáil questions from Deputy Austin Deasy:

"First there is an immediate need to protect the wreck from further unregulated tampering to ensure that the State's interest in both the paintings, if they exist, and in other artifacts with no known owner is protected… the Office of Public Works advised me today that it would be appropriate to place an Underwater Heritage Order on the site of the wreck. I have accepted this advice and asked that office to proceed with issue of the order. This has now been done and comes into effect immediately."
(Dáil Éireann Debate Vol. 448, No 1).

In a later Dáil debate on 2nd March 1995, he reiterated these points and also informed the House:
"I placed a heritage order on the site of the Lusitania primarily to protect the grave of the many people who lost their lives when the ship sank…"
(Dáil Éireann Debate Vol. 450, No 1).
The ownership of the objects and wreck is

determined under the terms of the Merchant Shipping (Salvage and Wreck) Act, 1993. While the hull, structure and appurtenances have been found to be the property of a private owner, other objects and unowned wreck are claimable by the Director of the National Museum of Ireland on behalf of the State as archaeological objects. By the mid-1990s, the National Museum of Ireland already had considerable experience with the archaeology of historic shipwrecks and the conservation needs of archaeological objects from maritime contexts. National Museum archaeologists had, for example, been involved in the State's High Court and Supreme Court cases concerning the ownership and regulation of diving activity on three Spanish Armada wrecks at Streedagh, County Sligo. The High Court findings in this case, *Re: La Lavia, La Juliana and Santa María de Visón*, served to extend the State's right to claim unowned archaeological objects from the sea (*King and Others v. The owners and all persons claiming an interest in the La Lavia etc. 3 I.R. [1999] 413*). This principle had already been established in *Webb v Ireland* (1988), the case concerning the ownership of the Derrynaflan hoard (*Irish Law Reports Monthly* 1988, 353).

Throughout the years, from the 1990s onwards, the National Museum worked with colleagues to consider applications and methodologies for diving operations on the site of the *Lusitania*. These included applications to dive only without raising wreck material or objects and more complex proposals for the raising of material by the owner Mr Bemis and his diving associates. In all cases, the Museum's approach was informed by the need for any objects raised from the site to be conserved professionally and then stored and/or displayed in a suitable Museum location. Licences to alter and to export archaeological objects retrieved from the wreck were required under the

Life jacket from the *Lusitania*. (National Museum of Ireland)

terms of the National Monuments Acts, 1930 to 2004 and the National Cultural Institutions Act, 1997 and staff of the National Museum of Ireland processed these applications.

During the past decade a number of court judgements upheld the principle of State ownership of archaeological wrecks found in territorial waters and with no known owners, particularly the findings of Mr Justice Herbert in *Bemis v Minister for Arts, Heritage, Gaeltacht and the Islands (2005)* which are clear concerning the respective responsibilities of the parties (O'Connor 2006).

Throughout this time, the National Museum of Ireland and the National Monuments Service actively engaged with the owner of the *Lusitania* in relation to licensing issues, always with the intention of coming to an agreement with Mr F. Gregg Bemis on his proposals to dive and to raise objects and wreck material from the site. In relation to the relative rights of the State and private owner, the judge found that "a balance must be found between the common good and property rights" and it has been the intention of the National Museum and other State authorities to proceed on that reasonable basis. While the State authorities must acknowledge the extent of private ownership of the wreck, statute regulations relating to the deposition and care of archaeological objects must also be observed. That has been a core part of the role of the National Museum in relation to the site and the objects retrieved from it.

The sunken remains of the *Lusitania* were found by Judge Herbert to be 'archaeological object' within the meaning provided in the National Monuments Acts and have been regarded as both monument and object from archaeological as well as legal perspective. In a key aspect of the judgement from the point of view of the National Museum of Ireland, it was found that: "the State has the right through the National Museum of Ireland to acquire any part of the remains of the vessel… properly considered necessary for the furtherance of scientific research or the advancement of public education in the State". It is worth noting also that Judge Herbert in the course of his judgement referred to the UNESCO Convention on the Protection of the Underwater Cultural Heritage, in which the State archaeological authorities have been involved.

The *Lusitania* is a significant part of the archaeological and historical heritage of Ireland as well as being of major international importance. The stories of those who travelled on her, whether surviving or meeting their deaths in the waters off West Cork, are encompassed in the remains of the once lavishly equipped vessel and the individual belongings of those on board – today represented as the remains of the wreck and the remains of individual artefacts within or around the wreck site. The importance of managing and protecting the wreck and its artefacts is perhaps best illustrated in the vivid first-hand account by survivor Ms Julia O'Sullivan. From near Kilgarvan, County Kerry but originally from Rosscarbery in County Cork, Julia told a visiting Schools Inspector in the 1940s:

"The *Lusitania's* saloon was longer and wider than a convent chapel and twice as beautiful, the ceilings covered with paintings and the walls divided by marble pillars and more pictures between the pillars; a rich carpet that would cover the soles of your shoes, over the whole floor and masses of live palm trees and flowers like you would see in Miami" (O'Connor 1951, 278).

The UNESCO Convention on the Protection of the Underwater Cultural Heritage and international best practice

While Ireland has not yet ratified the UNESCO Convention on the Protection of the Underwater Cultural Heritage, proposed changes in the National Monuments Act will enable it to do so once they come into effect. As a signatory to the Convention, Ireland supported its adoption at the UNESCO General Conference in 2001 (Kirwan & Moore 2011, 51). The principles enshrined in the Convention and in particular the rules of the Annex are adhered to in Ireland when dealing with its underwater heritage and the Convention closely reflects the existing national heritage legislation.

The centenary of WWI wrecks was reached over the period 2014–2018 and the 100-year rule automatically applied to these wrecks. It is also an important factor that UNESCO has focused its attention on the centenary and that the Convention on underwater cultural heritage has specifically addressed the submerged remains from that period. Noting that, with an estimated 6,000 wrecks from WWI lying under the seas across the world, a large number of which were the final resting place of those on board, the need to respect and protect these sites is obvious. UNESCO has called on all Member States and on society in general, to preserve these sites, affirming that they represent "a legacy which is at once a powerful reminder of war, and a convincing voice for peace" (www.unesco.org). As stated by Guérin *et al.* in UNESCO's publication, "This underwater cultural heritage is a major witness to history, but one that has not so far been comprehensively studied" (2015, 10). This is certainly relevant to the events that led to the sinking of the *Lusitania* and to the wreck itself.

Between 1995 and 2015 the wreck was protected by an Underwater Heritage Order and since then it is further protected by national legislation and also with respect to the international principles enshrined in the UNESCO Convention. With these protective measures in place any diving, research for archaeological purposes or investigative work carried out on the site must be undertaken in keeping with national and international best practice.

Protecting the Wreck, the Zone and its Dead

Since 1995 the National Monuments Service, in collaboration with the National Museum of Ireland, has been managing the regulation of activities on the

The exterior face of one of the first-class windows of the *Lusitania* recovered in 2011 by diver Eoin McGarry, under archaeological supervision by Laurence Dunne and Julianna O'Donoghue, still clearly shows the Regency style openwork pattern on the vent. Following professional conservation by Ian Panter of York Archaeological Trust, the quality of the workmanship, including the operating mechanism that still allows the window to open and close, was revealed. (Photo courtesy of Laurence Dunne)

wreck site. This has involved vetting dive licence applications, monitoring dives by officers of the National Monuments Service and licensing the recovery and conservation of artefactual material from the wreck site. By extension, there has been a need to liaise closely with colleagues in other departments on issues to do with the regulation of licensed activity, involving the Receivers of Wreck who are officers attached to Customs and Excise, Revenue Commissioners in the Department of Finance. Several Marine Notices have been issued for the wreck site over the years in collaboration with colleagues in the Department of Transport, Tourism and Sport's Maritime Services Division. These have included a notification in relation to the placement of the Underwater Heritage Order on the wreck in 1995, outlining the nature of the protection afforded to it; also a notice prohibiting fishing activity within the exclusion zone was issued in 2009 and a further Marine Notice was issued in 2011 notifying fishermen and other marine users that diving operations were

taking place at the wreck site. A close working relationship has developed between the National Monuments Service and the Irish Naval Service which has proven essential for policing the wreck site. The Naval Service has also facilitated the inspection of diving operations and Underwater Archaeology Unit monitoring of the wreck site in recent years. As a result of such close inter-departmental co-operation it is possible to police and protect the *Lusitania* and to have a realistic focus on developing a management and protection strategy for the wreck site.

The management strategy, however, is about more than preserving the historical and archaeological integrity of the wreck itself. The State is ever-mindful of the fact that the wreck site is the final resting place and an underwater tomb for hundreds of souls whose remains may lie sealed within it. The *Lusitania* is therefore also a war grave and deserves due consideration and respect as such. Any licence application or submission made in relation to any proposed activity on the wreck site, whether for

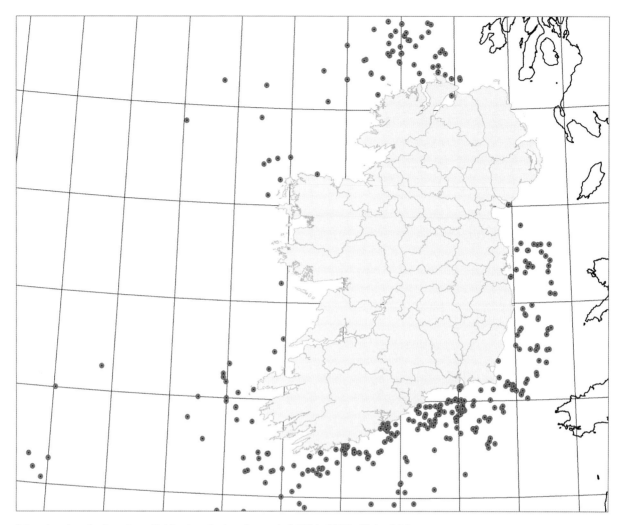

Map showing the location of ships lost during the period 1914–1918 off the Irish coast.

recreational diving purposes or with a research focus, needs to take account of the scale of human tragedy and loss of life that occurred there and of the evidence in that regard buried within the wreck, so that any such activity will be appropriate and sensitively carried out. This consideration, however, is not unique to Ireland or the *Lusitania;* there is a global concern that we should not only seek to respect and protect wrecks of historical or archaeological significance but that we should deal sensitively with wrecks that are also war graves. In Japanese culture, for example, there is a reluctance to investigate such wrecks or even to create images of them either by photography or other remote sensing methods (Jeffery 2006, 152–153) such is the respect for them as graves. Current discourse amongst heritage managers has identified this particular factor

as one of the more difficult challenges facing all nations with a maritime past (Delgado & Varmer 2015, 114), particularly when considering how best to give proper respect to such sites as graves while also considering them as potential heritage assets and tourist attractions (Guérin 2015, 121). The international community, under the auspices of the UNESCO Convention, is now actively looking at how best to recognise maritime war graves in international law (Forrest 2015, 126–134). Ireland, having its own management and protection strategies for the underwater cultural heritage, fully accords with these broader international efforts to ensure that such sensitive wreck locations are respected primarily as war graves.

Commemorating the Loss & Remembering the Dead

Lusitania 100 Cork Centenary Commemorations

The 7th May 2015 was the 100th anniversary of the sinking of the RMS *Lusitania* and all along the south-west coast of Cork, communities held ceremonies marking the event remembering those who lost their lives on that day a century before. While the county of Cork was the main focus of events, the sinking was also commemorated nationally and An Post issued a special stamp to mark the occasion. Internationally too, the sinking was remembered, with, for example, a major exhibition launched in the Merseyside Maritime Museum in Liverpool called '*Lusitania:* Life, Loss, Legacy'. Events were hosted in New York and

Irish Naval Service personnel forming a guard of honour at the *Lusitania* Monument in Cobh as part of the centenary commemorations marking the loss of the great liner. (Courtesy of Port of Cork Company)

President Michael D. Higgins inspecting the Naval Service guard of honour on 7th May 2015 as part of the centenary commemorations marking the loss of the great liner. (Photo Dan Linehan of the *Irish Examiner*)

Washington DC, linking into their wider commemorations on WWI, and in New Zealand a special commemorative coin was minted.

In Cork, a number of key events marked the day, not least the main commemoration ceremony in Cobh itself. Two others in Courtmacsherry and Kinsale – places directly linked with the events of 100 years ago – included poignant re-enactments that focused on the tragedy and the inquiries that followed the sinking. Presented below are elements from and overviews of the three key ceremonies held in Cork, including the full speech delivered by President Michael D. Higgins in Cobh.

Cobh: the Official Commemoration Ceremony

The official commemoration ceremony was held in Cobh, the town (then called Queenstown) where the majority of survivors and also remains of the victims of the sinking were brought following rescue and recovery. The Port of Cork Company, in association with Cobh *Lusitania* Centenary Committee and Cunard, organised the events. The funeral of the victims to the mass grave sites in Old Church Cemetery, Cobh, was re-enacted following the reading of victims' names by local children on the quayside. The Cunard liner *Queen Victoria* arrived and docked, having sailed by the site of the wreck itself to pay its respects, and wreaths were laid by passengers on board who were relatives of some of the victims of the tragedy. The official ceremony was attended by President Michael D. Higgins, who was accompanied

The Courtmacsherry lifeboat crew re-enact the launch and journey of the lifeboat *Kweiza Gwilt* 100 years previously to the scene of the tragedy. The original crew rowed the 12 nautical miles on a number of occasions to the stricken liner, having heard the explosion and having seen the ship sinking from the nearby Seven Heads Watch Tower. (Photo Dan Linehan of the *Irish Examiner*)

One of two commemorative stamps issued by An Post in 2015 to mark the centenary of the sinking of the *Lusitania*. This stamp shows the *Lusitania* under full steam. (Reproduced by kind permission of An Post ©)

100 Years On: Commemorating the Historic Wreck and Tragic Loss

Captain Michael McCarthy: Commentary on the commemoration ceremony of Lusitania 100th anniversary

On 7th May 2015, Port of Cork and Cunard together hosted a commemoration ceremony led by President Michael D. Higgins in Cobh to mark the centenary of the sinking of the *Lusitania*. Shortly after 7am, Cunard liner *Queen Victoria* arrived at Cobh cruise terminal with 2,144 passengers on board, on a seven-night 'Lusitania Remembered' voyage of which Cobh was the feature call. The vessel had stopped over the wreck site of the *Lusitania* at 03.30 hours en route from Southampton to Cobh where a wreath-laying ceremony took place led by the Chairman and Commodore of Cunard Line, David Dingle and relatives of passengers who had died in the tragedy.

Commemorations in Cobh commenced with the unveiling of four glass grave markers, commissioned for the centenary by the Port of Cork, at the Old Church Cemetery where the bodies of 170 victims of the *Lusitania* are buried in what were previously unmarked graves. The names of the victims have since been researched and are now inscribed on the new grave markers.

President Higgins arrived in Cobh town centre at 13.20 hrs to a full ceremonial guard of honour by the Irish Naval Service and proceeded to the town promenade where thousands had gathered. Following a welcome by the author, in my capacity as Commercial Manager of Port of Cork, the President

by a full Irish Naval Service guard of honour. He laid a wreath at the *Lusitania* monument. Further wreaths were placed there by the British, German and American ambassadors, the chairman of Cunard and the chairman of Port of Cork. The President gave a passionate speech that told the story of the ship, its loss and the significance of the wreck itself, including the Underwater Heritage Order that he had placed on it 20 years earlier in 1995 when he was Minister for Arts, Culture and the Gaeltacht. At the exact time of the sinking, 2.28pm, the liner *Queen Victoria* sounded its whistle and all in attendance contemplated in silence the shock, terror, loss and grief experienced by those at the scene of the sinking on that tragic day 100 years previously. The ceremony was co-ordinated by Captain Michael McCarthy, Commercial Manager with the Port of Cork and he gives his thoughts on the events here.

spoke about the tragedy of the *Lusitania* and its pivotal role in shaping American opinion on WWI. The whistle of the *Queen Victoria* sounded at 14.10 hours, marking the moment *Lusitania* was hit by a torpedo 100 years ago. Just 18 minutes later, a second whistle signalled the moment that *Lusitania* sank beneath the waves with the loss of 1,197 lives. During that poignant 18-minute period, prayers, music and words of remembrance were recited for the victims who drowned. Those gathered remembered that *Lusitania* is still a grave site for hundreds of people that went down with the ship. The catastrophe that unfolded off our coast and the trauma and loss of lives that ensued were brought home to those present during those sombre 18 minutes and the realisation that the victims were innocent people – men, women and children – with hopes and dreams just like ourselves.

Following the commemoration service in the town promenade, President Higgins laid a wreath at the *Lusitania* monument along with Commodore Rynd, Master of *Queen Victoria*; Kevin O'Malley, US Ambassador; Dominick Chilcott, British Ambassador and Wolfram Hopfner of the German Embassy. The commemoration concert continued during the afternoon and evening and concluded with a procession of over 60 small boats sailing from the harbour entrance to the town to re-enact the arrival of the recovered survivors and bodies from the wreck site.

Many relatives of those who died were in Cobh to remember their loved ones and to pay tributes to the efforts shown by the people of Cobh (then known as Queenstown) in the aftermath of the tragedy. The sinking of the *Lusitania* was a human catastrophe on a scale that the small town of Cobh had not experienced before or since and the commemoration was a very fitting tribute to all those who lost their lives. It was also an opportunity to remember a community that mobilised itself and helped survivors and the dead with such courage and compassion in the aftermath of this tragedy and their heroic response. What we do know is that on 7th May 1915 the rules of war were deliberately changed heralding an era in which there were no longer civilians, only targets, and the only thing that has changed across every subsequent war is the size and number of casualties.

The Port of Cork has fostered a 150-year relationship with Cunard and all three current Cunard vessels have visited Cork Harbour in recent years. We will never forget the lines and beauty of the now retired *QE2* that graced Cork Harbour over four decades. The *Lusitania,* however, has particular resonance with County Cork and Cobh in particular, in that so many of those who lost their lives and were recovered are buried here. Since 2007, whenever a 'Cunarder' calls to Cobh, the Port of Cork and Cunard have held a memorial service at the *Lusitania* monument and will continue to do so into the future.

Courtmacsherry lifeboat re-enactment
A series of commemorative events was held in Courtmacsherry and neighbouring villages in May 2015, including exhibitions of memorabilia relating to, and models of, the *Lusitania*, talks by local historians and an anniversary Mass. One of the central events, however, was a re-enactment of the launch and voyage of the lifeboat to the scene of the sinking. The crew of the RNLI lifeboat *Kweiza Gwilt* were the first to row out to the site on 7th May 1915, the explosion and sinking having been seen from nearby Seven Heads Watch Tower and the call going out for help. Leaving from the then lifeboat station at Barry's Point, near Blind Strand, some three miles east of Courtmacsherry where the present lifeboat is now stationed, it took them more than three hours to reach the scene of the tragedy. To commemorate this, Courtmacsherry lifeboat crew-members re-enacted the trip by launching a replica lifeboat from Blind Strand and rowing out to the *Lusitania* wreck site. On the strand were members of the local community and wider public, in period dress, lending atmosphere and further authenticity to the moment. Poignantly, a call had gone out to relatives of the original lifeboat crew and several family members were on Blind Strand and partook in the re-enactment (*Irish Times* 7th May 2015). A wreath was laid by the crew at the site in memory of the victims of the sinking but also in remembrance of their colleagues of 100 years earlier who were the first to rescue survivors and recover bodies. A fitting tribute to all involved.

Lusitania Centenary 2015
Mass Grave C

In eternal memory of the 69 victims buried in this grave

James Aitken Sr. • Margaret Armstrong Anderson
George Herbert Arthur • Catherine Symington Barr
May Barrow • Elizabeth Bull • Margaret Butler
Patrick Casey • Maud Gertrude Chirgwin
Ellen Crosby • Anna Davis • Cornelius Driscoll
Anna Enderson • Sheila Ferrier • Eva Eliza Finch
John Ford • William George Gardner • Catherine Gill
Charles Stuart Gilroy • Chastina Janet Grant
Samuel Hanson • Mary Hanson • Edith Mabel Henn
Kate Mary Hopkins • Elizabeth Horton
Sigurd Anton Jacobaeus • Liba Bella Jacobs
Mary Elizabeth Jones • Marie Kelly
Charles Lapphane • Issac Linton • Robert Logan
Alice Loynd • Timofej Lucko • Kenneth MacKenzie
Thomas Marsh • Stephen McNulty
George Peter Meaney • Walter Dawson Mitchell
John Henry Murphy • Mary Jane Press
James Roach • Joseph Robb • Annie Jane Roberts
George Ronnan • Minnie Smith
Thomas Edgar Stewart • William Stanford Thomas
Nina Tierney • Mary Tierney • Margaret Weir
Nina Wickham • Arthur John Wood
11 unidentified
males

Erected in

One of three inscribed glass memorial panels commissioned by the Port of Cork and Cunard and erected at the Old Church Cemetery in Cobh to mark the location where victims of the *Lusitania* are buried in what were previously unmarked graves. (Photo Connie Kelleher)

Kinsale commemorations and inquest re-enactment

Among the numerous scheduled proceedings to mark the sinking of the *Lusitania* in Kinsale, two events dominated. At the Old Head of Kinsale, Minister Simon Coveney officially opened the restored signal tower there, which is to be the location for a museum on the *Lusitania*. A commemorative plaque was also unveiled. In the town itself relatives of the 1915 jury later met the Minister ahead of a re-enactment of the Inquest. Held in the Court House and Regional Museum, students of the Kinsale College of Drama played out events that took place 100 years previous, including Captain Turner's testimony. Relatives of those who sat on the original jury sat in the same benches in the court house during the re-enactment. A Memorial Concert was also held in the medieval church of St Multose, to remember the victims of the sinking, and particularly those buried close by in the graveyard that surrounds the church. An exhibition on the *Lusitania* in the Regional Museum coincided with street events, a visit by the Courtmacsherry life boat and a wreath-laying ceremony at the Seaman's Memorial on Kinsale Pier.

Painting from the *New York Herald* and *London Sphere* published shortly after the sinking. The illustration wrongly shows a second torpedo striking the liner astern of the gaping hole left by the first and only torpedo strike. (Courtesy of the US Library of Congress)

List of Victims Buried in Old Church Cemetery, Cobh

The following provides the first comprehensive list of the 170 victims interred in the three mass grave sites in the Old Church Cemetery in Cobh, County Cork. It has been compiled by and presented here for publication for the first time through the generosity of Port of Cork Company which carried out the research work in advance of the 2015 commemoration ceremonies. The three main grave sites are listed – Mass Grave A, Mass Grave B and Mass Grave C – and the names published here have been duly inscribed on three glass memorial panels erected at the head of each of the respective grave sites by the Cobh *Lusitania* Centenary Committee in association with Port of Cork Company and Cunard.

Lusitania **Centenary 2015**

Mass Grave A

In eternal memory of the 24 victims buried in this grave

Mary Buchanan
Thomas Cain
Margaret Canigan
James Coady
Teresa Feeley
Clara Hebden
Margaret Drutler Jones
Francis William Lancaster
Daniel Lee
John Madden
Elizabeth Martin-Davey
Owen O'Hare
Patrick Sheedy
James Toole
Christopher Walsh
2 unidentified females and 7 unidentified males are also buried in this grave
Males unidentified, body nos 21, 149, 178, 204, 207, 236, 242
Females unidentified, body nos 27, 38

Lusitania **Centenary 2015**

Mass Grave B

In eternal memory of the 52 victims buried in this grave

Annie Thompson Bruno
Ethel Chambers
Margaret Coughlan
Nellie Fentiman
Edward Ferguson
Eva Mary Grandidge
Mr A. J. Greenshields
Clara Lee Groves
Thomas Hannah
Ernest George Henn
John Benjamin Hine
Sarah Hodges
Alice Eliza Hopkins
Jane Ellen Howdle
Isabella Gertrude Hunt
Margaret S. Kelly
Martha Maria Lakin
Lily Lockwood
Matilda Longdin
John V. Mainman
Stewart Southam Mason
Albert Palmer
Annie Palmer
Edgar Palmer
Archibald Ernest Parsons
William Quirk
Alice Ann Scott
Elizabeth Ann Seccombe
John Bowen Spillman
Anthony Stankiewicz
Albert Thompson
John Thompson
James Williams
Henry Edward Wood
12 unidentified females and 6 unidentified males are also buried in this grave
Males unidentified, body nos 68, 146, 185, 221, 222, 238

Females unidentified, body nos 43, 73, 109, 112, 113, 161, 167, 186, 224, 225, 226, 227

Lusitania **Centenary 2015**
Mass Grave C
In eternal memory of the 69 victims buried in this grave
James Aitken Sr.
Margaret Armstrong Anderson
George Herbert Arthur
Catherine Symington Barr
May Barrow
Elizabeth Bull
Margaret Butler
Patrick Casey
Maud Gertrude Chirgwin
Ellen Crosby
Anna Davis
Cornelius Driscoll
Anna Enderson
Sheila Ferrier
Eva Eliza Finch
John Ford
William George Gardner
Catherine Gill
Charles Stuart Gilroy
Chastina Janet Grant
Samuel Hanson
Mary Hanson
Edith Mabel Henn
Kate Mary Hopkins
Elizabeth Horton
Sigurd Anton Jacobaeus
Liba Bella Jacobs
Mary Elizabeth Jones
Marie Kelly
Charles Lapphane
Issac Linton
Robert Logan
Alice Loynd
Timofej Lucko
Kenneth MacKenzie
Thomas Marsh
Stephen McNulty
George Peter Meaney

Walter Dawson Mitchell
John Henry Murphy
Mary Jane Press
James Roach
Joseph Robb
Annie Jane Roberts
George Ronnan
Minnie Smith
Thomas Edgar Stewart
William Stanford Thomas
Nina Tierney
Mary Tierney
Margaret Weir
Nina Wickham
Arthur John Wood
11 unidentified females and 5 unidentified males are also buried in this grave
Females unidentified, body nos 6,15, 38, 81, 86, 100, 101, 103, 104, 120, 121, 128, 130
Males unidentified, body nos 10, 82, 83, 135, 15

RMS Lusitania: Past, Present and Future

The Fascination Continues

The ocean liner RMS *Lusitania*, in its heyday, was a ship of world renown and its wreck is no less renowned today. The wreck and the artefacts contained within and around it can tell a graphic story of the ship and its untimely demise by their simple presence on the seabed. The historical context of the ship itself is as one of over 1,000 vessels sunk in Irish waters during WWI. Since 2018 all of these wrecks now fall under the provision of the National Monuments legislation and the 100-year rule which affords them protection from unlicensed interference. The precedents set in relation to the regulation of activities on the wreck of the *Lusitania* will have wider implications for how the National Monuments Service deals with this added responsibility in the years ahead. Looking to the future there is a need for ongoing monitoring of the wreck and for scientific assessments to be carried out on its structural integrity so that informed decisions can be made in relation to striking a balance between preservation *in situ*, which is the ideal, and the need to rescue artefacts and key components of the wreck that could be lost forever as it slowly collapses in on itself. Archaeological studies and archaeological projects carried out on deepwater shipwrecks in other parts of the world highlight how best practice can be applied to even the deepest of archaeological sites. While in no way the deepest of wrecks, the depth at which the *Lusitania* lies is prohibitive to general diving limits on air and thus technical and commercial diving methods and deepwater technology will always have to be drawn upon to fully assess and explore the overall wreck site. When considering the recovery of archaeological objects from a deepwater wreck site such as the *Lusitania* (for example objects that might otherwise be lost as the wreck slowly collapses in on itself or more likely, that might be stolen by souvenir or treasure hunters) it is essential that normal archaeological procedures and principles should still apply. The high cost of such endeavours only strengthens the case in this regard as good planning can be the key to a successful outcome. For any such recoveries, therefore, detailed planning and preliminary archaeological assessments are essential to ensure the safe recovery of any material to the surface. The rules in the annex to the UNESCO Convention on the Protection of the Underwater Cultural Heritage are also quite clear in this regard and have the benefit of the shared experience and the efforts of many

Breeches buoy life ring from the *Lusitania*. Breeches buoy life ring was part of a rescue device like a zip line used to transfer people from a wrecked or sinking vessel to another vessel or ashore. (National Maritime Museum, Greenwich)

countries in developing appropriate strategies for exploring and investigating their underwater cultural heritage.

Recent work by the Irish National Seabed Survey/INFOMAR has enhanced our understanding of how the wreck is lying on the seabed and will form the basis for further targeted surveys that will help build upon this knowledge of the wreck and perhaps also answer some of the outstanding questions that surround its sinking. The mapping of these historic sites using high-resolution deepwater technology is providing essential support and critical information that is allowing investigation to the highest standards of archaeological best practice. The work of INFOMAR has presented the *Lusitania* in a new light, visualising and illuminating the site, providing key data that is allowing Government heritage managers to better protect the wreck site in keeping with its national and international significance. While making a significant contribution in their own right to our understanding and appreciation of the monument on the seabed, these images have provided a much needed and highly accurate baseline survey from which all future research can draw.

Additional information from individual divers to the wreck has been and will continue to be extremely

The *Lusitania* Monument in Cobh, County Cork. Designed and sculpted by internationally renowned Irish sculptor Jerome Connor (1874–1945). Connor won a prestigious competition in 1925 from the *Lusitania* Peace Memorial Committee in New York to design a monument commemorating the lives lost in the sinking of the RMS *Lusitania* (ssee www.buildingsofireland.ie for more detail). Initiated by Bert Hubbard, whose parents Elbert and Alice Hubbard lost their lives in the sinking, the commission was also financially supported by Gertude Vanderbilt Whitney, whose brother Alfred also perished when the *Lusitania* sank. Casting finally began in 1936 but with the outbreak of WWII, Connor went bankrupt and sadly died before its full completion. Following representation in 1965 by sculptor Domhnall O'Murchada, Assistant Professor of Sculptor in the National College of Art, the monument was finally completed in 1968 through the work of local sculptor Fred Conlon (1943–2005). (Photo Connie Kelleher)

important in aiding our understanding of the physical processes at play on the wreck, the adjacent debris field and the dynamics at work in the surrounding seabed. Members of the diving community are our eyes on the seabed, coming face to face with the *Lusitania* and its ghostly remains. It is they who can provide at first hand, personal insights into and valuable information on the condition of the wreck as it currently exists. They can observe the rate of deterioration and report back on issues that need to be addressed from a protection perspective, in particular vulnerable artefacts or parts of the ship's fittings that may be in danger of being lost or stolen. Through the statutory licensing mechanism, that considers all aspects of any proposed dive expedition to the wreck site, the collating of resultant data can contribute critical information for informing the ongoing management needs of the wreck site. Video and photographic imagery supplied by divers add to the existing corpus of information on the wreck and form part of the ever-expanding archive on the *Lusitania*, an archive accessible to everyone – the public, researchers, wreck enthusiasts and academics alike.

The wreck site of the *Lusitania* is now a living site, where marine organisms have taken up residence, retaining a curatorial eye each day on a wreck that is now their home. This natural element to the wreck site has untapped research potential and, looking afresh at the site as a living, natural heritage habitat, it can be seen as contributing in a positive way to our ocean ecosystem.

In commemorating the sinking of the *Lusitania* what must remain in the forefront of our thoughts is that the wreck, as it lies on the seabed today, is a monument to all who died on it and especially to those whose remains may still be entombed within it. It is also a reminder to all of the suffering and devastation that can be unleashed at the flick of a switch in time of war. The loss of life from the sinking of the *Lusitania* may have influenced political agendas and caused outrage across the world, but the personal impact felt on all levels, irrespective of class on board or profession on land, was most profound. The narratives relating to the Irish connected with the ill-fated liner may resonate locally but the true story of the *Lusitania* is one of human tragedy that touched millions of people around the world at the time; it continues to do so today when the accounts of those saved or particularly those lost are considered and pondered. It is incumbent upon us all to remember those lost, not to forget the events that led to that loss and to respect the wreck of the *Lusitania* as their final resting place.

It is hoped that this book will take its place as yet another tribute to those who lost their lives on the wreck, to those who came to the aid of the survivors and recovered the bodies of the victims and to the wreck itself. It was also written for those who are interested in its story and in preserving it as a reminder of the terrible consequences of war, in particular modern warfare when civilians are targeted more than ever and when terrible devastation can be inflicted in an almost casual fashion.

The wonderful images created by the Irish National Seabed Survey were the inspiration for this book and give us an opportunity to really engage with the wreck as it now is when reading the story that surrounds it. Many books have been written on the subject and many more will be; this is just another chapter in a never-ending story.

A Presidential Memory; a Presidential Tribute

In Memory of a Great Ship

The essence of the liner that was the RMS *Lusitania* may perhaps be comprehended best by reading a letter written in 1935 by President Franklin D. Roosevelt lamenting the end of service for *Lusitania*'s sister ship, RMS *Mauretania* (F.D. Roosevelt Digital Archives). Upon hearing that the *Mauretania* was to be scrapped, Roosevelt declared: "Every ship has a soul. But the *Mauretania* had one you could talk to. At times she could be wayward and contrary as a thoroughbred. Dislike to travel on her or not, the *Mauretania* always fascinated me with her graceful yacht-like lines – her four enormous black topped red funnels – her appearance of power and good breeding." He continued: "She had the manners and deportment of a great lady, and behaved herself as such." Roosevelt concluded by saying that rather than scrap the great liner after nearly 30 years of service "why couldn't the British have remembered the *Mauretania's* faithfulness – taken her out to sea and sunk her whole – given her a Viking's funeral, this ship with a fighting heart?".

The *Mauretania* was dismantled, completing its last voyage to the ship breaker's yard in 1935 where sections were recycled into munitions for the Second World War effort and other elements sold off to private individuals. Indeed the carved wooden panelled interior from the French Room of the Cunard liner can be seen in the Oak Bar on Dame Street in Dublin today, salvaged at the time of its dismantling and reassembled there. Even today, when enjoying the hospitality of that establishment, the sense of what it must have been like to sail in ships of such design and elegance is almost palpable.

Had the *Lusitania* not been sunk by a torpedo from the *U-20* and had seen out its days like the *Mauretania*, and likewise thereafter been consigned to the ship breaker's yard, there is no doubt that similar sentiments to those of President Roosevelt would equally have applied. It is the tragic events that surround the loss of the *Lusitania*, both before and after its sinking, that dominate the story of this great ship, with particular regard to the huge loss of life. Somewhat ironically, given Roosevelt's words, it seems a more fitting end for the ship itself to have finally come to rest within the very stretches of water upon which it majestically sailed than to have been broken up and sold off to the highest bidder after a long and faithful life of service. The sinking of the great liner, *Lusitania*, was a premature and lamentable end for a great ship although the circumstances of the sinking, huge loss of life and socio-political ramifications thereafter were undoubtedly the real tragedy. The fact that the ship remains a comparatively intact wreck in some small way goes to ensure that the integrity of this once great liner – its soul and its essence – is preserved for as long as it lasts on the seabed.

Where one President of the day grieved over the demise of the Cunard liner *Mauretania*, the President of Ireland, Mr Michael D. Higgins on the day of the centenary of the sinking of the *Lusitania* paid tribute to the loss of the great ship, those on board and also to the significance of the wreck that now remains.

President Michael D. Higgins' Commemoration Speech Centenary Commemoration of the Sinking of the Lusitania
Cobh, Cork, Thursday, 7th May 2015

Is mór an pléisiúr a bheith anseo libh inniu agus muid a comóradh céad bliain ó chuaigh an RMS *Lusitania* go tóinn poill. Is mian liom mo bhuíochas a ghabháil le Con Hayes dá chuireadh agus libhse ar fad as an fíorchaoin fáilte sin.

It is a great pleasure to be here with you today as we commemorate the centenary of the sinking of RMS Lusitania. I would like to thank Con Hayes for his invitation and all of you for that welcome.

Cobh, Kinsale and Courtmacsherry, are the three places most closely associated with this seismic and historic tragedy which claimed almost twelve hundred lives, including those of at least ninety Irishmen and women. All three towns played a heroic role in the event as lifeboats and local fishermen took part in the rescue operation and also brought to shore the remains of those drowned on that fateful day in May 1915.

Resting on the seabed the *Lusitania* constitutes a marine grave. It was that reason, with its related issues of due respect as well as its importance to Irish history and its wider international significance, that led to my decision, twenty years ago, as Minister for Arts, Culture and the Gaeltacht, to place an Underwater Heritage Order on the wreck. The sinking of the *Lusitania* is a critical chapter in the history of the First World War. The fact that 128 American citizens lost their lives is often cited as the catalyst for America entering the war in 1917. While this may not be quite the entire picture, it undoubtedly had a significant impact on American public opinion with regard to the war and on the resolve of President Woodrow Wilson who had intended keeping the USA neutral. America eventually abandoned its neutrality and entered the war on the side of the allies in April 1917; a decision which had the effect of hastening the end of the War, thus sparing many lives that might otherwise have been lost on the Western Front and elsewhere on the battlefields of Europe.

The sinking of the *Lusitania* is a story that has gripped the imagination of the world over the intervening decades and filled the pages of many books and articles in the years that separate us from that tragic day in May 1915. Some of those writings celebrate the significance of the *Lusitania* as a technical marvel of the age, reminding us of its place in the history of ship building and as holder of the Blue Riband for the fastest Atlantic crossings. Other authors have speculated as to its cargo and whether it was carrying armaments and if that might have contributed to the second explosion that may have led to the rapidity of its sinking.

Those are, however, stories for another day. Beyond the historical significance of this event, we come here today to remember the human tragedy of the 1,200 who died in the cold water of the Celtic Sea on a beautiful spring day in 1915. We remember the lives cut short and the futures and possibilities denied by the tragedy visited on unsuspecting voyagers who thought they were within safe reach of their destination when the *Lusitania* was torpedoed by a German U Boat.

From the accounts of the survivors, we have some sense of the almost unthinkable horror that they faced – a shortage of lifeboats, the injuries suffered from the initial hit and explosion, the desperation as passengers and crew tried to save loved ones, including the pathetic account of parents trying in vain to save their children, the treacherous flotsam and the violence of the rapidly sinking ship, and the dreadful wait for help in an ice-cold sea surrounded by the bodies of the dead. We come here today to think of those men, women and children, and of what they endured. I know that, joining us here this afternoon are over one hundred descendants of those who lost their lives as the *Lusitania* neared the coast of Ireland one hundred years ago. You represent the many families ruptured by that catastrophic event and remind us of the myriad human stories contained within the tragedy of the *Lusitania*.

We come here, too, to mark the courage and compassion of the people of Cobh, Kinsale and Courtmacsherry and of all those who undertook the rescue operation and managed to save the lives of the 700. And who also then recovered and cared for the remains of the dead. We remember the vessels which came to the aid of the victims, and especially those lifeboats who rowed out 12 miles to the site of the wreck in open sea, some on several occasions. We can only imagine the trauma which this tragedy brought to the town of Cobh, a town which of course knew well the perils of the sea, but which must still have been overwhelmed with the horror of a scarcely conceivable scale of death. There are so many stories of heroism and selflessness during the rescue operation that it is appropriate the people of Cork should be proud of how their ancestors responded to this terrible disaster.

All wars have their forgotten or unsung victims, those whose deaths do not bring forth posthumous medals or tributes. However, as we engage in a period of commemoration of World War 1, it is important that we not only focus on those who lost their lives on the battlefields and in the trenches, but recall the millions of civilians whose lives were also cut short during that cataclysmic period of world history. Some, like the casualties of the *Lusitania*, were the victims of deliberate acts of war, others died through malnutrition, famine and related disease. In whatever way they lost their lives, they were victims of a destructive, and indeed bewildering, world war, and their tragic deaths should not be reduced to that of collateral damage; it should be honoured and remembered with due respect.

Today we are also reminded that World War 1 was a war with a global reach, one that affected all areas of the European continent and many areas beyond.

Among the list of passengers and crew who perished that day were listed individuals and families from Canada, Britain, Russia, Norway, Persia and Belgium, reminding us that the wreck of the *Lusitania* is part of a global shared tragedy and heritage. As we recall today the individual stories of the passengers on this ship, we remember that during a four year period an estimated 17 million lives were lost to war, a war that was the product of political and diplomatic failure, and a war that failed to prevent further conflicts in Europe and other parts of the world, including the Second World War, which followed only a short few years later.

The importance of recalling the horror of war is that it should press us all to cherish and nurture peace, to defend the role of diplomacy, and seek to have it extended and reformulated to achieve peaceful resolution of conflicts. In recent weeks, I participated in the commemoration ceremony at Gallipoli, another dreadful episode of the First World War where Irish men including many from Cork, became the victims of a cruel and murderous war. Immediately after visiting Gallipoli, it was fitting that I also had the opportunity to visit our troops of today who are working in South Lebanon to support peace in that troubled land. At a time when the world is once again facing conflict and dispute in many regions, the urgency of the work of the making and maintaining peace between nations and peoples once again takes on a new importance. Ireland is a country that has known the horror and pain of war through our history, but it is surely one of our most significant achievements that since our independence we have sought as a nation to work towards peace, with peace-keeping lodged at the centre of our foreign policy.

Agus muid ag cuimhneamh ar an *Lusitania* agus orthu siúd a fuair bás amach ó chósta Chorcaí céad bliain ó shin, is é mo ghuí go ndéanfaimid tréaniarracht síocháin agus comhthuiscint a chothú idir gach náisiún.

In that spirit, as we remember today *Lusitania* and those who perished off the Cork coast a century ago, let us all redouble our efforts for peace and understanding between nations.

I would like to finish by thanking all those involved in the ongoing commemorations here in Cobh, where the Heritage Centre has a permanent exhibition dedicated to the memory of the RMS *Lusitania*, and also to those in Kinsale and Courtmacsherry for their hard work and initiative in keeping this important story alive for future generations to reflect on. I also wish the new *Lusitania* Museum project in the signal tower at the Old Head of Kinsale every success.

I will be meeting with representatives from that project shortly in Áras an Uachtaráin and I hope to visit when the museum is up and running. The magnificent bronze sculpture here in Cobh by Jerome O'Connor, to the victims of the *Lusitania*, is a lasting and fitting monument to those who died when that ship went down. As long as it lasts, together with the wreck on the seabed and the simple headstones in the Old Church cemetery and elsewhere, the memory of that day will not be forgotten.

For those who died one hundred years ago today, so close to our shores, might we finally say ar dheis dé go raibh a n-anamacha.

Go raibh míle maith agaibh go léir.

Diver Rez Soheil examining the telegraph head recovered by Pat Coughlan and his dive team during their licensed expedition to the wreck in July 2017 (Photo: Barry McGill).

Docking telegraph after being recovered by Pat Coughlan and his dive team in 2017 under licence and with archaeological supervision and oversight by the National Monuments Service (Photo: C. Kelleher, NMS).

References/Sources Consulted

Ballard, R. 1995. *Exploring the Lusitania*. Madison Press, Canada.

Bingham, B., Foley, B., Delaporta, K., Ryan, E., Mallios, A., Mindell, D., Roman, C. & Sakellariou, D. 2010. Robotic Tools for Deep Water Archaeology: Surveying Ancient Shipwreck with an Autonomous Underwater Vehicle, *Journal of Field Robotics*, 27(6), 702–717.

Bourke, E. 1998. Diving on the *Lusitania*. in *Shipwrecks of the Irish Coast*, Vol. 2, 932–1997; Dublin, 190–194, 204–208.

Brady, K., McKeon, C., Lyttleton J. & Lawler, I. 2012. *Warships, U-Boats and Liners*. Stationery Office, Dublin.

Brunicardi, D. 2012. *Haulbowline: The Naval Base & Ships of Cork Harbour*. The History Press.

Burns, G. 2012. *Commemoration of Death – the medals of the Lusitania murders*. Privately published.

Chatterton, E. K. 1934. *Danger Zone. The Story of the Queenstown Command*. Rich & Cowan. London.

Chatterton, E.K. 1943. *Beating the U-Boats*. Hurst & Blackett Ltd, Essex.

Church, R. & Warren D. 2008. Sound Methods: The Necessity of High-Resolution Geophysical Data for Planning Deepwater Archaeological Projects, *International Journal of Historical Archaeology*, 12, 103–119.

Church, R. & Warren, D. 2009. Deep-Water Archaeology in the Gulf of Mexico: A Multidisciplinary Approach, *Proceedings of US Hydro 2009*, Norfolk.

Cullimore, R. & Johnston, L. 2003. Rusticles Thrive on the Titanic, Ocean Explorer, National Oceanic and Atmospheric Administration, https://oceanexplorer.noaa.gov/explorations/03titanic/rusticles/rusticles.html

Dáil Éireann Debates:

http://oireachtasdebates.oireachtas.ie/Debates%20Authoring/DebatesWebPack.nsf/takes/dail19950125000019?opendocument&highlight=Lusitania

Damour, M. 2013. *Interdisciplinary Research at the Site of Three 19th-Century Deepwater Shipwrecks*. The Monterrey Shipwrecks, Bureau of Ocean Energy Management.

Dean, M. & Rowland, C. 2007. Visualising High Resolution Multibeam Shipwreck Data, paper presented at the US Hydro Conference in Norfolk, Virginia, The Hydrographic Society of America.

Delgado, J. & Varmer, O. 2015. The Public Importance of World War I Shipwrecks: Why a State Should Care and the Challenges of Protection, in U. Guérin, A.R. de Silva & L. Simonds, *Underwater Cultural Heritage from World War I*. Proceedings of the Scientific Conference on the Occasion of the Centenary of World War I, Bruge, Belgium, 2014; UNESCO, Paris, 105–116.

Dixelius, M., Oskarsson, O., Nilsson, O. & Rönnby, J. 2011. The Ghost Ship Exhibition: Frontline Deepwater Archaeology in the Baltic Sea, *Hydro International*, 15(1), 14–18.

Dunne. L. 2013. The Recovery of Artefacts from the RMS *Lusitania* and their Subsequent Conservation. Unpublished Draft Report submitted to the National Monuments Service, Department of Culture, Heritage and the Gaeltacht.

Dutton, P. 1986. Geschaft Uber Alles: notes on some medallions inspired by the sinking of the *Lusitania*, *Imperial War Museum Review*, 30–42.

Foley, B. 2010. *Deep Water Archaeology*. NOAA, Ocean Explorer.

Forrest, C. 2015. Towards the Recognition of Maritime War Graves in International Law, in U. Guérin, A.R. de Silva & L. Simonds, *Underwater Cultural Heritage from World War I*. Proceedings of the Scientific Conference on the Occasion of the Centenary of World War I, Bruges, Belgium, 2014; UNESCO, Paris, 126–134.

Gentile, G. 1999. *The Lusitania Controversies, Book 2: Dangerous Descents into Shipwrecks and Law*. G. Gentile Productions, Philadelphia.

GOM-SCHEMA: Gulf of Mexico Shipwreck Corrosion, Hydrocarbon Exposure, Microbiology and Archaeology Project.

Grant, R. 1964. *U-boats Destroyed – the effect of anti-submarine warfare 1914–1918*. Periscope Publishing. Penzance.

Guérin, U., de Silva, A. R. & Simonds, L. 2015. *Underwater Cultural Heritage from World War I*. Proceedings of the Scientific Conference on the Occasion of the Centenary of World War I, Bruges, Belgium, 2014; UNESCO, Paris.

Guérin, U. 2015. World War I Underwater Cultural Heritage and the Portection Provided by the UNESCO 2001 Convention, in U. Guéri, A.R. de Silva & L. Simonds, *Underwater Cultural Heritage from World War I*. Proceedings of the Scientific Conference on the Occasion of the Centenary of World War I, Bruge, Belgium, 2014; UNESCO, Paris, 117–125.

Hoehling, A. A. & Hoeling, M. 1956. *The Last Voyage of the Lusitania*. Bonanza Press, New York.

Irish Law Reports Monthly: http://www.westlaw.ie/

Jeffery, Bill 2006. The Federated States of Micronesia, in S. Dromgoole (ed.) *The Protection of the Underwater Cultural Heritage: National Perspectives in Light of the UNESCO Convention 2001*, Martinus Nijhiff Publishers, Leiden/Boston, 146–159.

Kirwan, S. & Moore, F. 2011. Update on Ireland and the UNESCO Convention on the Protection of the Underwater Cultural Heritage, in R. Yorke (ed.), *Protection of Underwater Cultural Heritage in International Waters Adjacent to the UK*. Joint Nautical Archaeology Policy Committee/Nautical Archaeology Society, 51–60.

King, G. & Wilson, P. 2015. *Lusitania: Triumph, Tragedy and the End of the Edwardian Age*. St. Martin's Press, New York.

Larson, E. 2015. *Dead Wake*. Doubleday Transworld Publishers.

MacLeod, I. D. 2002. In Situ Corrosion Measurements and Management of Shipwreck Sites, in C. V. Ruppé & J. F. Barstad (eds), *International Handbook of Underwater Archaeology*. Kluwer Academic/Plenum Publishers, New York, 697–716.

MacLeod, I. D. 2013. Monitoring, Modelling and Prediction of Corrosion Rates of Historical Iron Shipwrecks, in P. Dillmann, D. Watkinson, E. Angelini & A. Adriaens (eds), *Corrosion and Conservation of Cultural Heritage Metallic Artefacts*. European Federation of Corrosion, Woodhead Publishing Ltd, 466–477.

Martin, M. 2014. *RMS Lusitania: It Wasn't and It Didn't*. The History Press.

Maas, J. 1995, *The Sunday Press* (various articles)

The Irish Press, 23 January 1995, p. 11.

Massie, R. 2004. *Castles of Steel: Britain, Germany, and the Winning of the Great War at Sea*. New York, Ballantine Books.

Moore, F. 2012. *Lusitania*, in K. Brady, C. McKeon, J. Lyttleton & I. Lawlor (eds), *Warships, U-Boats and Liners*. Stationery Office, Dublin, 61–65.

Moore, F. 2015. One Hundred Years Since the Sinking of RMS *Lusitania*, Twenty Years Since it was Protected by Underwater Heritage Order, *Archaeology Ireland*, 16–19.

Molony, S. 2004. *Lusitania, an Irish Tragedy*. Mercier Press, Cork.

Negueruela Martínez, I., Belinchón, R. C., Sierra Méndez, J. L., Díaz Guerrero, J. I., Bruque Carmona, G. & Bermejo Martín, J. I. 2015. *El Pecio de Nuestra Señora de las Mercedes: Campaña de prospección y excavación de agosto de 2015 (profundidad 1136–1138m)*. ARQUA – Museo Nacional de Arqueología Subacuática.

O'Connor, J. 1951. *Hostage to Fortune*. M.F. Moynihan Publishing Company, Dublin.

O'Connor, N. 2006. Ireland, in S. Dromgoole (ed.) *Legal Protection of the Underwater Cultural Heritage: National and International Perspectives*, Kluwer Law, The Hague, 138–139.

O'Sullivan, P. 1998, 2014. *The Sinking of the Lusitania: Unravelling the Mysteries*. Collins Press, Cork.

Osborne, R. Spong, H. & Grover, T, 2007. *Armed Merchant Cruisers 1878–1945*. World Ship Society.

Peifer, Douglas C. 2016. *Choosing War: Presidential Decisions in the* Maine, Lusitania, *and* Panay *Incidents*. Oxford University Press.

Preston, D. 2002. *Lusitania, an Epic Tragedy*. Walker Press, USA.

Ramsay, D. 2001. *Lusitania, Saga and Myth*. Chatham Publishing, London.

Reeder, J. 2003, *Brice. The Maritime Law of Salvage*. Sweet & Maxwell Publications, London.

Rich, A. 1973. *Diving into the Wreck: Poems 1971–1972*. W.W. Norton & Company.

Salgado, A. & Russo, J. 2014. The History and Underwater Archaeology of World War I: The Case of the Operations of *U-35* off the Coast of Algarve, Portugal, in *Underwater Cultural Heritage from World War I*. Proceedings of the Scientific Conference on the Occasion of the Centenary of World War I, Bruges, Belgium, 24–36.

Sauder, E. 2015. *The Unseen Lusitania: The Ship in Rare Illustrations*. The History Press.

Simpson, C. 1972. *Lusitania*. Book Club Associates. London.

Simpson, C. 1983. *Lusitania: Updated Merseyside Edition*. Avid Publications, Liverpool.

Skoglund, F. 2014–2015. Vitenskapsmuseet Arkeologist Rapport 2014/5. Ormen Lange Shipwreck: Environmental Monitoring Project – Final Report.

Tolson, H. 2010. The Jacksonville 'Blue China' Shipwreck & the Myth of Deep-Sea Preservation, in G. Stemm & S. Kingsley (eds), *Oceans Odyssey: Deep-Sea Shipwrecks in the English Channel, Straits of Gibraltar & Atlantic Ocean*. Oxbow Books, Report 1, Oxford & Oakville, 145–157.

Viduka, A. 2007. Managing Threats to Underwater Cultural Heritage Sites: The SS Yongala as a Case Study, in R. Grenier, D. Nutley & I. Cochran (eds), *Underwater Cultural Heritage At Risk: Managing Natural and Human Impacts*. ICOMOS, 61–63.

Warren, M. D. 1986. *Lusitania: The Cunard Turbine-Driven Quadruple-Screw Atlantic Liner*. First published 1907 by Messrs. John Brown and Co. Ltd, Sheffield & Clydebank.

Warren, D. J. Church, R. A., Eslinger, K. L. & C & C Technologies, 2007. *Deepwater Archaeology with Autonomous Underwater Vehicle Technology*. Offshore Technology Conference, April 2007.

Warren, D. J. 2016. Acoustic Positioning and Site Formation on Deep-Water World War II Shipwrecks in the Gulf of Mexico, in M. Keith (ed.), *Site Formation Processes of Submerged Shipwrecks*, University Press of Florida, 235–248.

Wachsmann, S. 2011. Deep-Submergence Archaeology, in A. Catsambis, B. Ford & D.L. Hamilton (eds), *The Oxford Handbook of Maritime Archaeology*. Oxford University Press, 208–217.

Wood. M. G., Smith, D. I. & Hayns, M. R. 2002. The Sinking of the *Lusitania*: Reviewing the Evidence, *Journal of Science & Justice*, 42 (3), 173–188.

Wreck Inventory of Ireland Database (WIID) – Underwater Archaeology Unit, National Monuments Service, Department of Culture, Heritage and the Gaeltacht.

Newspapers and Magazines:

"Blue Ribbon of the Atlantic: Captured by the *Lusitania* all records broken", *Weekly Irish Times*, 19th Oct. 1907.

"The Sinking of the *Medea*", *The Times* [London, England] 27th March 1915: 9. *The Times Digital Archive*.

"The *Lusitania* Sunk", *The Times* [London, England], 8th May 1915: 9. *The Times Digital Archive*.

"Can the *Lusitania* be Raised? The Philadelphia Expedition – Naval and Salvage Opinion", *The Observer*, 14th May, 1922.

"American Passengers in the *Lusitania*", *The Times* [London, England] 13th May 1915: 5. *The Times Digital Archive*.

"The *Lusitania* Victims", *The Times* [London, England] 17th May 1915: 5. *The Times Digital Archive*.

"Another Liner Sunk with Loss of Life", *The Manchester Guardian*, 4th Jan. 1916.

"The *Lusitania* Crime: Germany's Latest Note to United States", *The Manchester Guardian*, 7th Feb. 1916.

"American Ultimatum to Germany", *The Manchester Guardian*, 20th April, 1916.

Lloyd's List 1900–1920, various newspapers; https://www.lloydslist.com

"*Lusitania*'s Alleged Cargo of Explosives: German Interest in Salvage", *The Manchester Guardian*, 1 July, 1922.

"Salvage Operations off Ireland", *The Times* [London, England], 28 Sept. 1935. *The Times Digital Archive*.

"*Lusitania*: The Epic Battle over its Biggest Mystery", 2014, Richard B. Stolley, *Fortune Magazine*, accessed online at: http://fortune.com/lusitania-gregg-bemis-legal-battle/

"*Lusitania* remembered in Courtmacsherry, Co. Cork", *The Irish Times*, 8 May, 2015.

http://www.irishtimes.com/culture/heritage/lusitania-remembered-in-courtmacsherry-co-cork-1.2198740

F.D. Roosevelt Digital Archives, http://www.fdrlibrary.marist.edu/archives/collections.html

* Newspapers accessed via: ProQuest Historical Newspapers: Trinity College Dublin Digital Archives.

Web Links:

http://www.Lusitania.net/index.htm

http://www.liverpoolmuseums.org.uk/maritime/visit/floor-plan/Lusitania/

www.rmsLusitania.info (Lusitania Resource)

http://www.boem.gov/Project-Overview/

http://www.boem.gov/SS4_GOMR-Monterrey_Shipwrecks/

http://oceanexplorer.noaa.gov/explorations/06greece/background/archaeology/archaeology.html

https://www.whoi.edu/sbl/liteSite.do?litesiteid=2740&articleId=4418

http://www.boem.gov/

https://hamdanlab.com/gom-schema/

https://www.titanicinquiry.org/Lusitania/

Index